Business Ethics

BUSINESS ETHICS

SECOND EDITION

THOMAS M. GARRETT

UNIVERSITY OF SCRANTON

RICHARD J. KLONOSKI

UNIVERSITY OF SCRANTON

PRENTICE-HALL, INC., Englewood Cliffs, New Jersey 07632

Library of Congress Cataloging in Publication Data

Garrett, Thomas M.
Business ethics.

Bibliography: p.
Includes index.
1. Business ethics. I. Klonoski, Richard J., 1952- . II. Title.
HF5387.G37 1986 174'.4 84-24927
ISBN 0-13-095837-9

Editorial/production supervision and
interior design: Shirley Stern/Nancy Fillmore
Cover design: Diane Saxe
Manufacturing buyer: Ed O'Dougherty

Printed in the United States of America

10 9 8 7 6 5 4 3 2 1

ISBN 0-13-095837-9 01

Prentice-Hall International, Inc., *London*
Prentice-Hall of Australia Pty. Limited, *Sydney*
Editora Prentice-Hall do Brasil, Ltda., *Rio de Janeiro*
Prentice-Hall Canada Inc., *Toronto*
Prentice-Hall Hispanoamericana, S. A., *Mexico*
Prentice-Hall of India Private Limited, *New Delhi*
Prentice-Hall of Japan, Inc., *Tokyo*
Prentice-Hall of Southeast Asia Pte. Ltd., *Singapore*
Whitehall Books Limited, *Wellington, New Zealand*

For Rosellen and Laurie

CONTENTS

II Relationship of the Firm to the Employee

III Relationship of the Employee to the Firm

PREFACE

This revised edition is the result of both pruning and expansion as well as of simplification and updating. Despite the changes and the addition of a coauthor, the purpose and the tone of the book remain the same. It is designed primarily for students and for those who have just begun a career in business. It does not provide an extended or detailed treatment of the social dimension. The reason is simple. Young people, beginning in business, do not have to make decisions in these areas, although they should be aware that they will have to face social problems as they advance.

The introductory character of the book is evident, not only in the delineation of subject matter, but in the method of presentation and in the simplified ethical theory which is provided. No attempt has been made to present a fully developed ethics that could be used in the study of problems of medicine and family life as well as in business. Rather, we have limited ourselves to a simple set of basic principles adequate for the problems met by beginners in business ethics. In other words, the theory is tailored to the purposes of this book and to the problems it studies.

In general, the reader will find no detailed catalogue of regulations, nor an exhaustive treatment of the topics selected for study. Our purpose has been to supply a minimum framework of business ethics. If the book sensitizes the reader to relevant ethical values and the way in which they can be brought to bear on concrete problems, it will have succeeded.

There are cynics who doubt the feasibility of even such modest aims as those listed. Indeed, the cynic thinks that business ethics is a contradiction in terms. The authors do not agree. Long acquaintance with many business people in both large and small businesses has convinced the authors that there are as many ethical business people as there are ethical teachers, physicians, and clergymen. Enlightened business people are sensitive to the dignity of their work, and to the needs of their employees and of society. They want to work out solutions that serve all legitimate interests.

It should be obvious that the amateur, or the incompetent, in business cannot live up to either the demands of business or the demands of ethics. It is hoped, then, that these pages will encourage not only ethical reflection but the study of business and business problems. Teachers in a variety of business courses will find that the matter can be used to introduce the student to the ethical dimension and to some of the problems in business that urgently need solution. In particular, these pages may convince the beginner that business is not a fixed and unchangeable reality but part of a rapidly changing world, which not only creates problems but offers an opportunity for technical brilliance and human creativity on the highest level.

TMG
RK

Business Ethics

1

SOME BASIC PRINCIPLES

INTRODUCTION

The word ethics is used in a rather precise sense throughout this book. It is important, then, to define the word and to distinguish it from terms with which it has sometimes been identified. Ethics is *not* the study of morals, whether this word is used to designate conformity to conventional social rules or the existing moral judgments of human beings. Although existing norms and judgments may contain valuable insights, ethics does *not* accept them but sets out to criticize and test them in terms of more ultimate norms. To put it another way, custom, convention, and the accepted courtesies of a society are *not* the foundations of ethics even though they can provide valuable hints as to what people think. For this reason, business ethics must study existing business codes to determine whether they have a solid foundation or only express a narrow consensus of a group or a sort of commercial etiquette.

Law enshrines many of the ethical judgments of a society, but it is *not* coextensive with ethics. In the first place, law is generally concerned only with the minimum regulation necessary for public order, while ethics examines both the individual and the social good in all dimensions. In the second place, ethics criticizes law as it does custom in an effort to obtain more perfect rules for the conduct of life. While the law demands great respect, it too is subject to the higher norms which ethics seeks to develop.

Although some will dispute the statement, ethics is *not* even identical with religious morality or moral theology. The great religions derive their moral precepts not only from human experience but from divine revelation. Ethics must rely on the unaided human reason. Because of this, the conclusions of ethics often fall far short of the ethical imperatives found in both Judaism and Christianity. Yet, there should be no conflict between ethics and moral theology, for ethics admits its incompleteness and sends religious people to their faith for the completion of moral equipment. No one should be surprised, then, if this short book does not use all the resources and equipment of the great religious traditions in moral science.

Since many people identify ethics with vague feelings of approval or disapproval, it should be noted that ethics does *not* rest on feelings but on the careful examination of the reality around us. It may be unpleasant to fire a man, but ethics may demand just this. It may be hard to do the right thing in the face of strong disapproval and at great personal cost, but principles and not emotions should guide us. With all of these things in mind, we can now make some more positive statements about the nature of ethics.

Ethics is the science of judging specifically human ends and the relationship of means to those ends. In some way it is also *the art of controlling means so that they will serve specifically human ends.* From this point of view, ethics involves the use of any human knowledge whatsoever which has something to tell us about the relations between people or about the suitability of the possible courses of action. As an art, moreover, it involves techniques of judging and decision making as well as the tools of social control and personal development. Thus, ethics really is or should be involved in all human activities.

Business ethics is concerned primarily with the relationship of business goals and techniques to specifically human ends. It studies the impacts of acts on the good of the individual, the firm, the business community, and society as a whole. While it does not concentrate on the obligations which a person has as a private individual and a citizen, these enter in since the business person is not three separate people. This means that business ethics studies the special obligations which a person and a citizen accepts when he or she becomes a part of the world of commerce.

The social dimension of business ethics must not be overlooked since many major problems arise from the relationship of business to the broader society. Often, as we shall see towards the end of this book, business is involved in social situations which harm people or breed injustice even though business alone is not responsible for this. Unless we recognize this social dimension from the very start, there is danger of reducing business ethics to a study only of individual relationships between human beings. This would simplify the work at hand, but only by robbing business of its full human significance.

SPECIFICALLY HUMAN ENDS

In speaking of specifically human ends, we must avoid a narrow point of view. Humans are complex beings existing in an extremely complex world. While we may be tempted to work out some simple answers, experience shows us that such answers are not only frustrating but at odds with the way people actually see themselves. Humans are not merely creatures made for power or pleasure. They want and are made for more than this. They are not purely and simply social beings but have worth and dignity as individuals. All aspects of the human being enter into ethics. The problems, of course, arise when we have to harmonize the seeming conflicts between the person's various roles. This may be difficult, but dodging the issue does not solve the problem.

Since this is not a book in general ethical theory, we shall merely present a brief, but broad view of the specifically human ends in ethics. Because this view coincides in a large part with the American political tradition and with the teaching of great religions as well as with the view of a large number of modern philosophers, it is hoped that the reader will at least accept it as a working hypothesis.

The specifically human goal is the full human perfection of the human being as person. This means that the person is not a means to the perfection of society, the state, or anything else. In this view, societies are means to the real perfection of the individual even though they may contribute to this only indirectly. Societies, of course, are very important means, and the individual who harms a social good can injure countless individuals. It is important, then, to make careful distinctions lest individuals think that societies exist for them alone and not for all individuals. Although the person as a person is to be treated as an end, some of his possessions, talents, and activities must be subordinated to others. An individual's work, for example, may be used as a means to the good of a company providing that personal dignity and essential well-being are respected. So too, a man's time and wealth may have to be sacrificed to society, so long as the person himself is not reduced to a mere thing. The full significance of this will emerge as we develop the difference between the necessary and useful goods, and the major and minor evils that can occur in human life.

There are gray areas where it is difficult to say whether or not the person, or merely some accidental aspect, is being used as a means. However, reflection and experience can clarify these areas or at least reduce them to manageable dimensions. One hundred years ago we could not see clearly that most forms of segregation were really insults to basic human dignity. Today, most intelligent people see the evil of segregation quite clearly. Similarly, there was a time when employers considered any contract as just, even though it might involve the brutalization of the worker and his or her family. Thus, ethics has as one of its functions the sharpening of our knowledge about the work practices affecting the dignity of the individual human being.

It should be noted that much unethical activity is rooted in a lack of respect for our own personal dignity. People who see their worth as identical with their earning power will tend to look at everyone else in the same way. The result is often a neglect of the rights of those who must work with or for such a person. Concretely, then, an understanding of ethics demands an appreciation of what it means to be truly human. This understanding is not easily attained, for momentary desires and narrow views of self-interest blind people not only to their own best advantage but to the rights of others, and to the exigencies of the societies of which they are a part and to which they owe so much. If a person does not have this breadth of vision, this book cannot give it to him or her. At very best, a book can only enlarge one's outlook a little and show how the basic respect for humanity is to be expressed in actual business situations.

Those who have a fairly complete idea of what it means to be human will see at once why it is necessary to be ethical and to study ethics. The reason is not that good ethics and good business always coincide. Business efficiency, after all, is only one part of life. The reason is ultimately found in the fact that both the study and practice of ethics contribute to our growth as human beings and to the growth of society as a fit place for humans to exist. Unless we have an ethics that puts business into the total framework of both individual and social life, we may end up as "successful" business people but mediocre, if not morally crippled, persons. Since mere instinct and vague good will are not enough to guide us in the complicated world around us, the study of goals and means is necessary.

RESPONSIBILITY IN A GENERAL SENSE

Whatever hurts individuals or the institutions necessary for their growth may be looked upon as an evil in some way. Similarly, whatever truly promotes the growth of individuals and the means available to them is a good. Such simple statements, though true, will not solve our ethical problems. Nearly everything we do has some harmful impact on ourselves or others. If we were responsible for all the evil that flowed from our activities, whether foreseen or not, we would despair of ever being ethical. Even the most conscientious advertisers know that some silly people will be deceived by their carefully written copy. Are such advertisers, on that account, unethical? Similarly, the employer who must fire an incompetent knows that the individual's family will suffer. Is the employer responsible for these effects?

The answers to these questions are found in the very traditional ethical theory which states that "human beings are responsible at least for what they freely will whether as a means or an end." To a large extent, this theory is found in civil law as well as in ethics. Someone may ask, however, if this means that I have no responsibility for the evils that I foresee will flow from my actions as necessary, probable, or possible effects. Is a drug manufacturer who foresees that some people will be killed by his or her drug excused from all responsibility on the grounds that he or she does not will their death as a means or an end? The answer is obviously no; for both common sense and ethical theory recognize some obligation to avoid even unintended evil consequences in some circumstances. Where, then, do we draw the line?

TYPES OF EVIL AND CONSEQUENCES

At the very start, we must recognize that there are different types of evil consequences. Some evils strike at the very dignity of the human being or at means which are necessary for human growth. If one destroys an individual's health so that he or she cannot work, one has done that person a serious harm. On the other hand, there are evils which destroy goods that are only useful. Thus, if an individual loses a job, he or she has not, in most cases, lost his or her livelihood completely. It would appear to be simple common sense that the greater the foreseen but unintended harm, the more responsible a person is liable to be. However, if one is responsible for all the evil though unintended effects of one's actions, life would be impossible.

In an attempt to solve this problem without falling into the vicious theory that the end justifies the means, writers on ethics have evolved the following principles. First, one is responsible for whatever one wills as a means or an end. *If both the means and the end one is willing are good in and of themselves, one may ethically permit or risk the foreseen but unwilled side effects if, and only if, one has proportionate reason for doing so.* There is a proportionate reason if the good willed is equal to or greater than the evil permitted or risked. To put it another way, one is not responsible for unwilled side effects if one has a sufficient reason for risking or permitting them, granted always that what one does will as a means or an end is good.

This principle is so crucial that it needs considerable explanation if it is to be used properly and not as a cover-up for unethical conduct. It does not imply that the end justifies the means, for the means willed must be good before the principle can be used. One cannot use it to justify deliberately killing an innocent person even if this action would save thousands of lives. An individual cannot steal another person's property even though this will enable him or her to make millions of dollars. At best, the end can supply that person with a sufficient reason for permitting or risking *side effects which are not means* to the end. One may catch pneumonia by diving into an icy stream in order to rescue a child, but the pneumonia does not help that person to rescue the child. It is not a means, and it may be permitted or risked for such a serious reason.

The words *permitted* and *risked* have a precise meaning which reinforces what has been said above. One permits an evil when one foresees it as *certain* but does not will it as either a means or an end. One risks an evil when one foresees it as *probable* but does not will it as either a means or an end. In short, there is no question of risking or permitting what is willed as means or end. When in doubt, ask yourself whether you can obtain your end even if some miracle were to stop the evil side effects. If the answer is yes, the evil is probably not a means. If the answer is no, the evil is a means and the principle of proportionality or limited responsibility does not apply.

Honest business people use this principle constantly. The advertiser who has prepared his or her copy carefully foresees that a few stupid people will misread it. Such an advertiser is not unethical, however, for he or she does not will their stupidity, and the service rendered to thousands allows him or her to permit the stupid to suffer. It would be quite different, of course, if this advertiser willed to deceive them as a means of keeping business going. In such a case, the business person can have no proportionate reason because he or she is using an evil act as a means.

The principle given above is still very crude. It needs to be refined if it is to be truly useful in making decisions. In the first place, it is necessary to have more precise norms for judging proportionality. In the second place, it is necessary to investigate more carefully a special case involving minor evils.

PROPORTIONALITY

Proportionality is to be judged by

1. The type of goodness or evil involved
2. The urgency of the situation
3. The certainty or probability of the effects
4. The intensity of one's influence on the effects
5. The availability of alternate means

In the abstract, a necessary good will outweigh a merely useful good. The more necessary will take precedence over the less necessary. For example, something necessary to keep a business in existence will take precedence over a cut in the ordinary dividend. Note that the hardship worked on some stockholders is not a means since of itself it does not help the company.

In the concrete, necessity is influenced by the urgency of the situation. Thus, staying in business today involves both research and the ability to meet one's payroll. However, since research can be postponed without irreparable harm, it would take second place to meeting the payroll because both the company and the employees depend on this for their existence.

The *certitude or probability of an effect* must be considered since a serious harm which is only slightly probable can clearly be outweighed by a certain good. Every major business innovation involves some risk of serious financial loss. The risk can be justified, however, if careful calculations indicate a high probability of increased growth. So too, work involving the risk of physical harm can be justified by the necessity of earning a living. Note that the risk of physical harm is not a means but is undesired by everyone.

The *intensity of one's influence* can be considered since often something or someone else is the major cause of the evil side effect. In firing a man for absenteeism, the employer foresees some hardship in the family. The major cause is not the employer but the employee whose faults created the situation. When one's influence is minimal, it does not require a very great good to justify permitting the side effects. Here again the hardship worked on the family is not a means for it does not help the company at all.

All of these *factors must be considered together* in making a judgment about proportionality. In general, one can start with the first factor and work down to the last, totaling up the factors at the end. Sometimes even this method will not yield an absolutely clear decision, but it will at least narrow the area of doubt.

The availability of alternate means must be considered. If the good effects can be obtained by a method which involves lesser evils or no evil side effects, it would be irrational and therefore unethical not to choose the alternate means, all other things being equal. One does not fire a worker if some lesser disciplinary action will produce the desired results, nor does a person permit others to be deceived if a little extra work will remove the cause of the deception. It would be irrational and unethical to continue an economic system which was inefficient when it was possible to work toward a better system which costs no more. This means that the possibility of alternatives which realize the good with fewer unwanted side effects can create an obligation to work towards this system. The *status quo* is not a perpetual excuse for permitting evils that can be eliminated.

MINOR EVILS OR PHYSICAL EVILS

The principle of proportionality applies to the risking or permitting evils of all sorts. It can be used only when what is willed as means or end is good. What, however, are we to say of the following cases where common sense tells us the act is ethical even though it involves willing some evil for a proportionate reason?

A parent spanks a child in order to teach him or her that stoves burn. An employer docks the wages of someone who is consistently tardy in the hope that the loss will reform the worker. The government destroys millions of tons of wheat to support prices. In each case, an evil—the destruction of good—is willed. In each case, most will feel that there is a proportionate reason for doing so. Does the end justify the means in these cases?

Writers on ethics have attempted to solve this problem in various ways. Many distinguish between a *physical evil*, which can be willed for a proportionate reason since it does not harm the dignity of humans, and a *moral evil,* which involves willing something that is at odds with that dignity. This distinction is useful if one remembers that more than a physical evil is involved when the rights of others are concerned. Thus one cannot steal another's property on the ground that the money is only a physical good and its loss only a physical evil. A doctor cannot cut off a man's arm to save his life if the man objects.

It is also possible to distinguish between *major evils*, which involve the destruction of goods necessary for an individual or society as well as the violation of rights, and *minor evils*, which involve harm to a purely physical good or to some means that is useful, but not necessary, for the individual and society. This distinction, too, is not without its difficulties, for Americans tend to evaluate things in quantitative terms whereas rights are qualitative. Furthermore, whether one uses the distinction between physical and moral evils or between major and minor evils, it may take years of study to determine the exact nature of some acts and effects. Indeed, much of this book is an attempt to decide what evils are major and therefore unethical when willed as means or ends.

No matter what distinction or terminology is used we can say: It is unethical to will a major or a moral evil either as a means or an end. Secondly, a physical or a minor evil cannot only be permitted or risked but can even be willed as a means if there is a proportionate reason. The reason is that the physical or minor evil by definition does not go against the essential dignity of humanity but promotes it when there is a proportionate reason. As a result, the physical or minor evil is really not a full-fledged evil in many situations.

PROBLEMS

In the world of business, as elsewhere in human life, it can often be difficult to decide whether we are dealing with a major or minor evil. In addition, there is the danger of considering any harm done to others as minor and any good for ourselves as absolutely necessary. As a result, good ethics demands that individuals make a continual effort to arrive at objective evaluations of the effects of their acts on individuals and societies. The neglect of this obligation is certainly a source of much unethical conduct and might also be considered a major problem in ethics.

A few examples will help to illustrate the dangers of subjectivism divorced from objective considerations. An employer is installing a new process which is very dangerous. There are safety measures available, but the employer does not use them, since their cost will reduce profits which will be higher than the industry average. Here we are dealing with an unethical act, since the potential harm outweighs the loss of some profits. One might be tempted to call the risk to life a purely physical evil, but it is more than this since workers have a right not to be *unnecessarily* exposed to risk, while a company has no right to a profit, let alone a high profit, gained by exposing others to unreasonable risks.

A young accountant tampers with his records to conceal his own mistakes. This fudging will almost certainly lead to costly errors being made. He argues that he will lose his job if caught and so is ethically justified. Actually, there is no question of risking or permitting here, since he is willing an evil as a means. Furthermore, by his contract, he has agreed to take the consequences of his mistakes. Finally, the harm to the company would outweigh the harm to himself even if he were not using an unethical means to escape penalties. Even if the harm to the company were relatively small in terms of dollar losses, the employee is violating his contract which gave the company a right to honest work. Injuries to contracts are not minor, for the whole fabric of business and society depends on their sacredness. For all of these reasons, the young accountant is doing something unethical, no matter what his own rationalizations may be.

Additional dangers of self-deception exist when the impact of an act is not directly visible and so not ordinarily considered. This is particularly true of the harmful effects on the spirit of society as a whole or on the morale of a company. A company may not see the hardship worked on people by the cumulative effect of over-pricing or false advertising, but it is there and must be considered. It may be difficult to estimate the effect of a plant relocation on a local community, but it cannot be disregarded as a minor consideration.

Law, custom, and public opinion do not completely determine the ethicality of our actions, since they are more liable to be concerned with minimal requirements than with the complete situation. However, all three can be valuable in arriving at an evaluation of impact. In addition, they can help the business person escape some of her or his very natural bias.

Law in particular is important, since it enshrines the careful thinking of society's best representatives. At times it may be out of date, since law often lags behind the developing social situation. However, although the law may permit things which are unethical, in general what it forbids is also forbidden by sound ethical thinking. For these reasons, the study of business law and consultation with lawyers should be considered as a necessary preliminary in most areas of business ethics. If later chapters do not give complete summaries of the law on given points, it is because a short book must assume that the reader has other sources of information.

While trade customs often embody the results of sound ethical theory, they must be examined with care. The custom may have developed to protect the interests of only one group involved in business with the result that sometimes they sanction or even command acts which may be harmful to other groups. Thus, although untruthful comparisons of products are unethical, advertising that avoids all meaningful comparisons with competing products is certainly not in the best interests of the consumer. No matter what the custom in the area, the ethical business person will want to examine it for all of its implications.

Public opinion too, needs to be studied carefully. Often it condemns or approves certain business practices because it is unaware of the real issues involved. At the same time, it will often indicate to the ethical business person that he or she has overlooked some relevant factor. The same remarks apply even to the writings of the "professional" critics of business who, though often ill-informed, may have something valuable to say.

What we have said above may be summed up in the following:

1. It is unethical to will a major evil to another or to one's self whether this evil be a means or an end.
2. It is unethical to risk or permit a major evil to another or to one's self without a proportionate reason. A proportionate reason ex-

ists when the good willed as means or end equals or outweighs the harmful side effects which are not willed as either means or end.

3. It is unethical to will, risk, or permit a minor evil without a proportionate reason.

POSITIVE OBLIGATIONS

The brief statements made above provide analytic tools for the determination of what we must avoid as unethical. In addition, we have positive obligations, that is, duties to bring something into existence. In a most general sense, we have a positive obligation when something is necessary for our own human perfection, the dignity of others, or the necessary operations of society. These obligations or duties are not absolute since the urgency of one may cause the postponement of another. In more general language, an individual may often have proportionate reasons for not fulfilling a positive obligation at a given moment. This makes positive obligations very different from the negative obligation to avoid all unethical acts as defined above. Thus, the extreme need of workers for their wages may excuse a manager temporarily from paying a dividend. The obligation to pay wages at a certain level may even be mitigated by the obligation to keep the business in existence, since the firm may be necessary for at least the subsistence of a large number of people. Because each general and particular situation must be judged in terms of the four factors covering proportionality, more general rules cannot be given at this time. It should be obvious, however, that positive obligations are limited by the following factors.

One is not obliged to do a good act whose harmful side-effects outweigh the good effects intended. Indeed, one is forbidden to do such an act, since one has no proportionate reason for permitting the harm. A person is thus not obliged to raise wages when this will destroy the firm and put hundreds out of work within a short time.

One is not obliged to help individuals who will not help themselves, although one may do so if one desires. A company does not have to keep an employee who refuses to get proper medical care or to follow company regulations. A firm may have no obligation to contribute to local institutions if these are badly run.

A person is not obliged to perform a positive good act if someone else has a more primary obligation and is willing and able to fulfill it. A firm, for example, is not obliged to provide for the education of workers' children since the workers and the government are in charge of this. Obligations, in other words, do not come into existence merely because there is a need, but they are assigned according to some system. The problems arising from the nonassignment or from the new assignments of responsibilities will be touched on in later chapters. Obviously, where there is no clear assignment many, if not all, will try to pass the buck to others. On the other hand, the social assignments of new responsibilities often create confusion and tension in the business community. Affirmative action in hiring and firing is an example of this and will be treated in Chapter Three. The problem of absolute liability in Chapter Nine arises out of the need to involve business more deeply in the solution of social problems. The assignment is, however, not necessarily a complete success.

RIGHTS

The term "rights" will be used frequently in the following pages. It derives its meaning from what has been said above. Basically, a right is a claim on other people. It arises from the relationship of the individual to some good which is either necessary or useful for his perfection. Since we are all human beings, these claims must be respected, for we cannot disregard another's good without in some way injuring ourselves. Rights, however, are not all of a piece, nor are they unlimited. In a general sense, we can distinguish between quasi-absolute rights, which are claims to things that a human needs in order to be a human, and relative rights, which are claims not to be unreasonably impeded in the pursuit of even useful goods. While it is not always easy to differentiate between these in the concrete, the theoretical distinction is a useful analytic tool.

A person who is forced to work twelve hours a day, seven days a week, can hardly remain human in the long-run. To force this person into such a situation is to violate his or her right to be treated as a human being. On the other hand, requiring people to appear for work at a given hour may limit the search for some useful good, like an extra hour of sleep, but it is a reasonable limitation and does not make the worker less human. It is reasonable to make workers wear safety helmets even though they may dislike hats. It is unreasonable and a violation of freedom to make workers in an office wear hats. These examples are trivial, but it must be remembered that freedom is a good, and one needs a proportionate reason for limiting it.

It may be difficult to determine the exact limits of a right. On the surface, the violation of a right may appear to be no more than a slight injury to the feelings, property, or freedom of another. In reality, the violation of a right involves the denial of the claims of human dignity. It involves placing some mere thing or desire above the human person. Since all of us have basically the same nature, one harms oneself when one harms another. One twists one's sense of values when one disregards rights, and in the long-run, this can destroy an individual as a human being no matter how much he or she may appear to gain by the careless and ruthless refusal to consider the claims of other people.

Some rights are inborn; a person has them merely because he or she is a human being. The right of life is a prime example. Other rights, however, come into existence only when some act has created a title to a particular thing. A person has a right to a plot of land only if he or she has bought it, received it as a gift, or received it as a part of an inheritance. Similarly, in most cases a person has a right to a particular job only after a contract has been made.

This point is extremely important, for although a person may have a right to work, no particular individual has a corresponding obligation to employ him or her. In short, there are some rights that are claims against society as a whole rather than against particular individuals. When this fact is overlooked, serious harm can be done by trying to force obligations on people against all reason. Only society itself can ultimately decide which individual, if any, must fulfill these claims against society itself. Often the assignment is made by law, but as we shall see, it can often be made by ratifying the acts of those private individuals and firms who freely decide to undertake the job.

The exercise of rights, whether absolute or relative, is limited by the rights of others, and by my obligation to respect them, as well as by my obligation to respect myself. A person may own a house, but he or she has no right to burn it down when this would endanger his or her neighbors. Even if there were no neighbors, a person would be limited by the obligation to use material things intelligently. An employer has a right to hire whom he or she will, but this is limited by his or her obligation to respect the human dignity of others. A person has a right to life, but he or she may not save his or her own life by killing an innocent person. A company has a right to trade, but it has no right to exploit its customers. In short, the exercise of rights involves us in the concrete world where concrete possibilities, as well as the rights of others, limit the legitimate extent of our own claims. To put it another way, one's obligation to respect others conditions one's legitimate claims to things and on people.

COOPERATION IN EVIL

Many cases in business ethics involve cooperation in evil. When this cooperation includes willing the evil, either as a means or an end, this is an unethical act except in those cases where there is a proportionate reason for willing a minor or physical harm. At times, however, one can be involved in a situation against one's will. If a person does not will the evil either as a means or an end, that person may have a proportionate reason for risking or permitting harm. For example, the secretary who is typing up fraudulent reports is cooperating in an unethical act. Ordinarily she does not want others to be deceived or to profit from it. Further, if there is little that she can do to stop the harm while she needs the job, she can continue to do the physical work of typing. Since many cases of this type will appear frequently later on, it will suffice to say that the same basic principles apply here as elsewhere in ethics.

A treatment of the power of example is important in business ethics, for studies have shown that the example of the superior or supervisor is very significant for the other workers. As a result, bosses must see that their acts do not encourage others to engage in unethical conduct. This is a delicate situation, for harm may be done if the employee misinterprets even an innocent act. Often, then, it is necessary to avoid both unethical conduct and the appearance of it. It should be clear, however, that when the superior's act is actually ethical, he or she can permit or risk the harm for a proportionate reason. After all, the stupidity of others does not create an absolute claim on the behavior of a person of true good will.

LOCATION OF RESPONSIBILITY

Our remarks about cooperation and bad example should make it clear that we can be partially responsible for actions whose primary cause is found elsewhere. Even though another may bear the major responsibility, I can share in it. Adolph Eichmann was responsible for his acts even though Hitler gave the orders and common soldiers performed the actual murders. In short, the ignoble art of buck-passing should not obscure the fact that we are responsible for our share of the evil when we risk it or permit it without a proportionate reason.

Often, to be sure, we are in a position where we cannot prevent evil or can prevent it only at a disproportionate price. In such situations, we may be excused temporarily. More often than not, the obligation is transformed into the duty to work for the correction of the underlying situation. A minor employee often has no way of stopping his superior from stealing, but he can make the thefts more difficult. In these cases where he cannot stop the evil, he is at least obliged to mitigate it.

THE GRAY AREAS

There are gray areas in business ethics as in the rest of life. Neither our knowledge of the facts nor our analytic tools are accurate enough to solve all problems immediately and clearly. Despite this, ethics can help us in reaching correct decisions in the vast majority of cases. The science of ethics, then, has very high utility even though it is not perfect. The gray areas themselves are not excuses for unethical conduct so much as challenges to our intelligence. Thought and study can remove much of the darkness and narrow the gray areas to a very small proportion of life. Indeed, because intelligence is one of the necessary means to the perfection of the individual and society, we have a real obligation to study ethics and to bring the murky areas into the light of reason. Progress may be slow here as elsewhere, but the difficulty of the job does not excuse us forever.

BY WAY OF SUMMARY

The seemingly simple idea that good is to be done and evil avoided becomes complex when applied to the world of business affairs. In most cases, consequences and intentions are relevant concerns regarding the determination as to whether the good to be obtained is proportionate to the evils permitted or risked.

Many contemporary writers on ethics tend, however, to focus either on consequences or on intentions. While some ethical problems are clearly best attacked from the perspective of consequences and others most fruitfully analyzed by examining intentions, the vast majority of ethical dilemmas encountered in business require *both* the weighing of consequences and the scrutiny of intent.

10

2

ECONOMIC AND POLITICAL CONSIDERATIONS

INTRODUCTION

The principles developed in the previous chapter apply to all humans and all human actions. The business person, however, is not only a person and a citizen but a manager of a group with a specific purpose. As a result, business people have obligations which arise specifically from their role as business people. Since these obligations are additions to their basic duties, such obligations form the proper matter of business ethics. In theory, the specifically business obligations can be derived by applying basic principles to particular business situations. In practice, the beginner is unable to do this effectively, since he or she is liable to overlook important factors.

The present chapter, then, introduces some general considerations about the economic and political functions of managers. These considerations are necessary for the proper application of principles to the myriad problems which occupy the remainder of this book. While the relative importance of these factors varies with the size of the firm and its position in relation to the economy as a whole, they are involved in nearly all business situations.

THE PURPOSE OF THE FIRM

From *society's point of view* business firms exist to supply useful goods and services at a reasonable cost. From the *individual's* point of view the business firm may exist to supply income, power, prestige, creative satisfaction, or a combination of these. From society's point of view, a manager is obliged to run the firm efficiently within the limits set by law and ethics. It should be noted that society can and does change its definition of reasonable costs and therefore its definition of efficiency. The new attitudes about industrial health, pollution, product safety, and even gasoline mileage are all the results of society's changed ideas of what constitutes a reasonable cost for a product. Occasionally, society even changes its definition of what constitutes a useful good or service. The changing attitude towards smoking is an example of this.

So long as the individual motives of those involved in the firm do not distort or destroy the social purpose of the firm there need be no problem in business ethics even though some motives create problems in personal ethics. To be more concrete, even profit as an individual goal need not be in conflict with the social purpose of producing goods and services at a reasonable cost.

To the extent that the manager realizes the social goal of efficient production of goods and services designed to satisfy human needs and desires for useful goods, he or she should show a profit. Profits, though they motivate some individuals, are not the goal of the firm itself so much as a *possible* measure of its performance. The word *possible* in the previous sentence is important, for a profit can result from luck, fraud, coercion, or from exploitation of ignorance and irrationality, as well as from economic efficiency. Profits, in brief, are ambiguous both ethically and economically. For this reason, we prefer to say that the manager business person is obliged to be efficient rather than obliged to make a profit.

The necessity and hence the obligatory character of human economic efficiency needs to be stressed. On it depends not only the survival of the firm but the livelihood of employees, owners, and managers. Moreover, the ability of people to satisfy needs and useful desires depends on efficiency so long as even some means are scarce. This very pragmatic approach should not shock anyone, providing the idea of human economic efficiency is not narrowed artificially. Efficient management demands long-run as well as short-run maximization. It stresses careful use of physical resources, worker morale, executive development, research, and good relations with the community and the society at large. Each one of these factors is a means to the end which cannot be neglected if the firm is to do its job. Each one of these factors also has impacts on human beings which cannot be disregarded, since the manager of a firm is a person who must respect the dignity of others. What must be stressed is the fact that the firm is not a philanthropic or charitable institution. It is a tool, a group organized to serve a very specific end, and its purpose cannot be disregarded without great harm to society and individuals.

It should be noted that the specific purpose of a firm or corporation is not inalterable. In Chapter Fourteen, we shall return to some of the problems involved in determining what the corporation must do and be tomorrow. For the present, we shall content ourselves with a simple and manageable concept of efficiency in the production and distribution of economic goods and services in a market economy.

THE SOCIETAL NATURE OF THE FIRM

If the firm is to attain its end and realize its goals, all people involved must cooperate. In short, a firm is a society that cannot realize its purposes without human cooperation and a unity of purpose. In the firm, as elsewhere, this cooperation is not automatic but is created by managers. It is for this reason that managers have to plan, organize, and control the activities of people so that the firm will prosper. This means that the manager fulfills his or her obligations to individuals largely by fulfilling his or her obligations to the firm. The manager is not free to subordinate the good of the firm to one or two individuals since this harms dozens, hundreds, even hundreds of thousands who depend on the firm for their livelihood and need-satisfaction.

In political terminology, the manager is an authority who is in charge of the public good and social weal of a firm. This good is as dependent on the contributions of members as the members are dependent on the distribution of the goods of the firm. The social good of the firm, however, is not identical with the good of the members.[1] This social good is composed of various factors which have the following characteristics:

1. They are produced by the cooperation of many people.
2. They belong to the firm and not to any member no matter what the law may say.
3. All members benefit in some way from the existence of these factors.

Thus, the social good of a firm comprises not only physical equipment, patents, and contracts, but good will, morale, loyalty, the unity of the managerial team, and its reputation. The manager is in charge of producing and combining these factors so that the firm can attain its goal. To the extent that the manager succeeds, he or she will provide contributors and workers with income and other satisfactions. If the manager fails, both consumers and employees suffer. Even if stockholders own the company, in the sense that they have a right to a share in the liquidation, it should be clear that they do not own the social good, since most of it would disappear in a liquidation. For all practical purposes, stockholders are most accurately treated as remote contributors rather than as owners. We shall return to this point in Chapter Twelve when treating the firm's relationships with stockholders.

[1]This view of the public or common good is well developed by Thomas E. Davitt, S.J., in *Elements of Law* (Boston: Little, Brown, 1959). Real insight can be gained by reading Yves R. Simon, *Philosophy of Democratic Government* (Chicago: University of Chicago Press, Phoenix Books, 1951), pp. 1-71.

THE RIGHTS AND OBLIGATIONS OF MANAGEMENT

The obligation to manage the firm gives rise to the right to manage. To put it another way, the basic authority of the manager arises from his function. This is true even in the case where the manager is the sole owner. His property right may give him control over various things, but it does not give him authority over workers, their time, and energies. He obtains this latter right by means of the work contract which binds the employee to cooperate for the good of the firm in return for definite benefits.

While the work contract is the source of most managerial authority, it is unfortunately so vague that it can and does give rise to many disputes concerning the exact limits of management rights. In an age when employers had the power to enforce nearly all of their desires, it was assumed that management had all rights not explicitly denied by law or the work contract. In the day of unions, however, it is assumed that management has only such rights as are explicitly given it by formal agreement. In short, newer thinkers would claim that management operates on the basis of rights delegated either by the owners or by the workers. Moreoever, in this view of things, management is not the sole interpreter of the terms of the delegation.

Although this question is of the utmost importance, it cannot be fully developed in a short book. For the present then, we will discuss certain limits on management authority and consider practical suggestions for the removal of gray areas.

In the first place, management authority is certainly limited by its purpose—the good of the firm. A manager does not have the right to use the firm as a personal toy. Even though he has the *power* to subordinate the good of the firm to his own personal profit or whim, he does not have the *right* or authority to do so. This limitation can be applied to cases concerning the use of insider information and to conflict of interest cases as well as to the area involved with executive compensations, stock options, and expansion plans.

In the second place, management authority is limited by the clear rights of workers, stockholders, suppliers, dealers, and the community at large. Since most of these rights are relative, the line is not always clear, but it is there somewhere under the smoke and haze. As a result, the ethical manager must constantly ask whether his or her act is a reasonable interference with another's search for even useful goods. The employer, for example, should look long and hard at orders or policies which interfere with the home life of employees, their political activity, personal privacy, and freedom to change jobs.

A manager may limit relative freedom for reasonable cause related to the good of the firm, but it is not always easy to decide what is reasonable. Moreover, since we tend to exaggerate our own interests and minimize those of other people, correctives are needed. A free contract which specifies and limits can be a useful aid in this area. A contract, however, really helps only if it is free and not the result of power positions, fraud, and ignorance. Custom too may be a guide to what is reasonable and unreasonable, but it is not decisive since conditions change and demand the readjustment of both contracts and customs.

While there are many undefined areas where there is no clear objective demarcation between the rights of management and the rights of other groups, this does not automatically give management the right to make unilateral decisions which can change the work contract by interpretation. This can be seen by comparing the management process to the legislative process in the political order. There are differences between them, but the similarities are great enough to be significant.

In the political order, experience has shown us that unilateral decisions by power holders constitute a threat to individual rights and freedom. As a result, power has been institutionalized by a constitution that provides for due process and a system of checks and balances. Thus, the legislator is supposed to hear all points of view; the executive must answer to the courts; and the courts must observe procedures designed to reduce arbitrary decisions. Behind our political institutions is the realization that rights and obligations cannot be unilaterally determined but must reflect the various interests involved. Those who created our judicial system also recognized that the arbitrary application of even a basically just law may lead to injustice in the long run.

We suspect that, in the business world, much of the dispute about management rights is really a dispute about the way in which decisions are made and enforced rather than about the right of management to make them. In short, there is a suspicion that what people fear is not management authority but management power that is not checked by an institutional framework providing for both bilateral decisions and due process. The problem cannot be solved without some form of corporate constitutionalism.

No matter what stand one takes in theory, in practice sound management would demand that attention be given to the reasoned opinions of those affected as well as to the development of a system which removes suspicion of arbitrary application. Much of this already exists in the area of collective bargaining, but as we shall see in later chapters, much remains to be done to insure justice on the management level itself.

Much of this may sound foreign to the ears of the rugged individualist, but such a person should be realistic enough to see that one rules only by the consent of the governed. If that consent is extorted or forced, we are dealing with tyranny, whether in a nation or a corporation. The manager is also sitting on a powder keg when there is no real assent to his or her authority. On the other hand, when the consent is freely given and the work contract mutually acceptable, a climate will exist in which trust and mutual confidence reinforce productivity as well as fair dealing.[2]

[2]The reader is referred to the thesis of Douglas McGregor in *The Human Side of Enterprise* (New York: McGraw-Hill, 1960). See also Thomas J. Peters and Robert H. Waterman, Jr., *In Search of Excellence: Lessons from America's Best-run Companies* (New York: Harper and Row, 1982).

THE FIRM AND ITS ECONOMIC RELATIONSHIPS

The business person's rights are limited not only by the rights of his or her own employees, but by those of the various groups with whom he or she must deal. Thus, business people must consider the impact of their decisions on stockholders, suppliers, dealers, competitors, customers, unions, local communities, and on the economic system as a whole. This is merely to say that the firm is part of a total economic and political system and not an island without foreign relations. Like employees, the economic groups that deal with or are affected by the firm have rights which must be respected.

The rights and legitimate claims of the various groups connected with or related to the firm are not always clear. The manager, indeed, must mediate between these claims, seek to reconcile them and to maximize the good of the firm and the system of which it is a part. This is not merely a question of justice but of business efficiency, since the firm cannot long exist without the continued cooperation of all these groups. Sometimes a firm can exploit another group, but in the long run, the good of the firm is bound up with the interests of all its claimants.

While it may not be easy to determine what is fair in each and every case, the manager must realize that power, fraud, ignorance, and passion can vitiate the relationships of justice and even destroy the system of exchange and cooperation. The manager must, then, continually distinguish between what he or she can do because of his or her power, and what is fair when all factors have been considered. This, after all, is the meaning of responsible self-regulation.

BUSINESS POWER AND THE BROADER SOCIETY

The problem of power and the limits of authority within the firm bring us to the relationship between the firm and the broader society. While this topic will be discussed in greater detail toward the end of the volume, certain remarks should be made here and now in order to provide at least a framework for discussion. This is particularly important, for some readers might think that the ethics of the firm involve only individuals and economic groups such as stockholders, suppliers, dealers, and competitors.

In classic economic theory, the optimum relationship between a firm and the good of the whole society was supposed to be established automatically. As a result, business people did not have to worry about broad social impact. The classical theory, however, rested on assumptions which are no longer true, if they ever were. Modern business people must face problems of national policy if they are to fulfill their duties as citizens. It is not easy to delineate these duties or to assign precise responsibilities, but there can be little doubt that they do exist.

In line with the principles governing proportionality, business people must certainly seek to minimize the harmful impact of their activities. Realistically, however, they often are not in a position to do this except by entering into cooperative arrangements with the industry, the unions, and the government. As a result, many of the business person's obligations in this area are really transformed into a general obligation to work with others for the betterment of society. This, as we shall see time and time again, means that he or she must accept their responsibility as a citizen and transcend the *status quo* and the accepted practices of business in the past. It does not mean that the business person must become a social reformer on a large scale or turn their business into a benevolent association. Neither activity would really serve society in the long run.

In order to arrive at a new perspective on his relation to the broader society, the business must consider some of the facts of life which differentiate business today from business a hundred years ago. The principal fact is that of power and of society's attitude toward it.

No society can be indifferent either to the fact of power or to the way in which it is used. It must be concerned not only with actual misuses of power but with potential misuses as well. There are several reasons for this. In the first place, power is not ethically neutral. Secondly, power must be made to serve society and all human beings. Finally, the protection of rights involves control of the power to abuse rights.

Power is not ethically neutral, even though it is often said that we may judge it by its uses and the techniques used to generate it. Certainly, the uses and methods of generating power have ethical significance, but so does the fact of power itself. To put it another way, ethics is concerned not only with intentions and the foreseen effects of power, but also with its inherent tendencies, which may not be recognized by those who wield power.

Lord Acton felt that power corrupts and that absolute power corrupts absolutely. While this may be an overly pessimistic view of the inherent tendencies of power, the statement contains a great deal of truth. It is a truth that has been confirmed by the lessons of history and considered by the framers of the American Constitution who designed a system of checks and balances. We do not know exactly how power corrupts, but it seems to intoxicate and convince people that its mere possession justifies their acts and frees them from the ethics of the weak and powerless.

It should be noted that the dangers inherent in power apply to government power as well as private power, to union power as well as to business power. As a result, there is need for a continual reevaluation of all institutions designed to control power in a society. Just as we examine the functioning of our political machinery to see if it serves the people, we must examine our economic system with the same end in view. Without constant surveillance and scrutiny, there is no guaranteed way to preserve freedom, protect rights, and direct the forces of society to worthy goals. Slogans will not do the job, nor will power struggles designed to advance the interest of one group at the expense of another.

In our present American situation, business must admit that it has great power which is less than perfectly channeled in its responses to the needs of society. Sometimes this power is gained because the business community faces unorganized and uninformed consumers. Sometimes it exists because the lobbies and the public relations department of business are better equipped to influence legislation than is the general public which is so often inarticulate and ignorant. Possibly the greatest source of power lies in the pooled intelligence and resources of the business community. No matter what the source of the power, society cannot be indifferent to either its actual or potential uses. It follows that business people must also be interested in these questions if they are to be good citizens as well as efficient handlers of the society's resources.

Because this is a book for beginners, limited space is given to the consideration of these vital social questions. They exist, however, and must be answered if the nation and the business community are to prosper.

THE HIERARCHY OF GOALS

The previous pages place managers, whether they are owners or agents, at the center of a network of relationships to persons, groups, and things. By the very nature of their jobs, they must, for both business and ethical reasons, consider the impact of their actions on all to which they are related. They must seek to reconcile claims within a framework that recognizes the rights and needs of both individuals and groups. This is a very large order. It cannot be filled unless the manager has real technical competence and a well thought-out hierarchy of goals.

There is no ready-made formula that gives each goal a precise place in relation to the dignity of the human person. The golden rule may help to form sound ethical attitudes, but it cannot be applied without recognizing the demands of concrete situations. What is a just decision today may be an unjust decision tomorrow if key conditions have changed. A goal which must take a high place today may have to be subordinated tomorrow. At best, then, only some general considerations can be given. The manager can use these in applying the methods of the first chapter to the problems he or she meets in business.

The quasi-absolute rights of real persons take precedence over the claims of either the company or the general society. This is to say that the person as such may never be directly and deliberately subordinated to the good of any group. The reason is clear. Groups exist to help individuals and cannot justify deliberately willing the destruction of the person. Fortunately, the temptation to use a human being as a mere thing is fairly rare in modern business, so this first rule of precedence should not have to be invoked too often.

This should not cause us to overlook the fact that this rule of precedence can be violated. The firm which forces an employee to act against his conscience is subordinating an absolute and inalienable right of a person to the company. The companies which once worked men six days a week, ten hours a day, in deep mines certainly subordinated the person to the company in effect, if not in intent. Perhaps workers had proportionate reasons for taking such risks, but it is difficult to see how the companies did. Although a person may not be used as a means that is directly and deliberately subordinated to the company, there can be and are sufficient reasons for asking a worker to freely risk even his or her life once all precautions have been taken. The work of high steel erectors and sand hogs is inherently dangerous, but it is not necessarily unethical to hire people for such jobs.

Conflicts about relative rights can be settled in favor of a party whose rights are clearly spelled out in a contract. Where there is no such contract or where the contract is not a truly free agreement, the dispute can often be resolved by examining the reasonably founded expectations of the parties involved. Where neither policy, custom, nor accepted practice gives a clue to what is a reasonable expectation, fairness seems to demand that either collective bargaining or outside arbitration be used lest selfishness dominate.

By contract, the claims of workers to their wages takes precedence over the manager's desire to expand. By custom, if not by law, the need of the firm to expand will take precedence over the claims of stockholders to a dividend. There are, however, no rules for deciding whether the demand of workers for a wage increase over a fair wage will take precedence over the claims of stockholders. It is for this reason that bargaining and arbitration are necessary lest the issue be settled by power alone. On the other hand, in a conflict between the workers' need for wages which are decent and the stockholders' desire for a dividend, the worker would take precedence. Wages are the basic income for workers, while dividends are generally only relative goods for most stockholders. In theory too, stockholders have agreed to take risks, while workers have not.

The needs of the nation take precedence over the needs of the firm, but what is merely useful for the nation does not take precedence over what is necessary for the functioning of the firm. Ultimately, the decisions in this area of conflict have to be made by the government, but the rule can guide the business person in his or her attitude toward the passage of new laws.

All of this comes down to saying that business ethics is far more complicated than the simple interpersonal ethics we learned at our mother's knee. This should surprise no one who understands management, for the function is complicated by its nature. This complexity, however, may help to explain why outsiders fail to realize the true problems of the businessperson and why insiders are often afraid to face the true challenge of business ethics.

Ethics is necessary, but it is not sufficient to insure justice in societies, whether they be corporations or political entities. There are many areas of life and business where there are no ready-made answers. Often, fairness will depend on the existence of free contracts which create order where none existed before. Free contracts, in their turn, need the support of society and law which prevents one party from dominating another. In addition, there are other areas where so many people have an interest that fairness demands that all parties be represented and that society itself assign obligations and draw up rules to establish order where none exists by the nature of the case. Ethics can help in providing general guide lines, but it is no substitute for that creative decision making that is an essential function of human social life. No one should be disappointed if ethics often points up problems without being able to give a definitive solution.

These last remarks should serve to reinforce the importance of social institutions that protect rights and enable people to realize their potential. Good will and an enlightened conscience are not enough unless they can be expressed in effective institutions. We may say that there is a general obligation to work for the creation of such systems and rules as will promote the specifically human end of which we spoke in Chapter One. It is for this reason that the truly ethical person will give full consideration to the harmful effects of his or her acts upon society and to the need for perfecting the society itself.

BY WAY OF SUMMARY

Society expects business firms to produce and distribute useful goods and services at a reasonable cost. The managers who are charged with this have rights and obligations which both come from and are limited by society as a whole and by the firm itself. Thus, business ethics like business itself takes place in a social context where the power of business and the power of government must both be moderated in the interests of society as a whole and the quasi-absolute rights of real persons.

3

HIRING AND FIRING

INTRODUCTION

The ethics of hiring and firing are governed by the dignity of the applicant or worker, by the contractual relation between employer and employee, and by the purpose of the firm. The personnel manager and policy makers must guard against discrimination, breach of contract, and decisions that are not conducive to efficiency and worker morale.

As a general rule, the firm hires people in order to increase its production and productivity. Family companies may want to supply jobs to relatives, but even here the efficiency of the operation must be considered lest the firm, its employees, and the general public suffer harm. The ethics of hiring is largely governed by the norm of efficiency as it was outlined in Chapter Two. A woman is hired for the benefit of the firm and should be selected on the basis of her ability and willingness to serve the social good of the company and the public.

The manager who hires the best people available within the limits set by the firm's salary scale and recruiting budget is acting ethically. If the manager discriminates between applicants, it must be on the basis of job-related qualifications. This obligation arises not only from his or her basic duty to the firm but from the manager's obligation to treat people equally in those areas where they are equal. To act on caprice or prejudice is to act irrationally and unethically. In short, selection on the basis of factors that are not job-related is both an insult to human dignity and a failure to serve the firm.

These basic duties were incorporated into the Civil Rights Act of 1964 and subsequent amendments and related legislation. The law admits that religion, sex, race, national origin, age, and handicap can be bona fide job qualifications in some very rare and carefully defined situations. In general, these factors are not of themselves relevant. Race and color are never legally admitted as bona fide job qualifications. While it might be possible to imagine very special cases where race and color might be relevant to a job, the law is generally sound. Moreover, even from an ethical point of view any alleged exceptions should be viewed with the greatest suspicion.

The law extends the area of ethical obligation, for it excludes some of the ethical exceptions that could otherwise provide temporary excuses. In the absence of the law, for example, an individual might hesitate in hiring a black because he or she anticipated serious trouble from his or her prejudiced employees. Today such a fear does not excuse employers affected by the law. Others must make sure their fear is well-grounded before they can invoke the prejudices of third parties as a temporary excuse for discrimination in hiring practices.

DETERMINING JOB QUALIFICATIONS

Both ethics and the law demand that managers define concrete, bona fide job qualifications. This is a difficult task but a necessary one. It involves the suitability of the applicant for the immediate job and his ability to profit from training for more important positions. Considering the cost of hiring and training workers, the potential for advancement is certainly a bona fide employment qualification. Unfortunately, the judgment of potential can also be a disguise for prejudice with the result that the law does not necessarily recognize the ethicality of such judgments.

When job qualifications have been determined, the manager must apply his policy intelligently. He or she must decide on the combination of interviews and tests and check their predictive value. While the law permits the use of professionally developed tests if there is neither intentional nor actual discrimination, the conscientious employer will recognize that pencil-and-paper tests may discriminate against culturally deprived groups.[1] This will not necessarily be unethical discrimination. If the job demands skill in reading, writing, and arithmetic, it is certainly not discriminatory to use professionally developed pencil-and-paper tests. On the other hand, if neither the immediate job nor the training for future jobs demands such skills, the tests could be unfair in effect if not in intent. Similarly, the pertinence of vocabulary level, cultural knowledge, and the like are to be judged in terms of the jobs to be filled. Since this is easier said than done, many firms avoid tests altogether.

The problem is relatively simple in screening applicants for ordinary industrial jobs. Unfortunately, jobs that involve the handling of people demand qualifications that are intangible and cannot be revealed by standardized tests.

[1]There will be many problems of interpretation in this area, but the issue will always be whether or not the discrimination is relevant to job qualifications. Employers, however, should watch court decisions carefully.

General culture, voice, diction, poise, and the ability to socialize are all relevant to a great many jobs, yet they are subject to considerable vagueness of definition. Even when such factors are not decisive, they are important plus values. In some cases, the factors are so important that companies will spend time and money entertaining not only the applicant but his wife to discover their suitability to the company. The use of such criteria is ethical if there is no discrimination based on qualifications unrelated to the job. Once again great care is necessary since social class, gender, and cultural biases may cause an employer to overvalue superficial qualities which have no substantive relationship to the job.

THE USE OF STATISTICS

Many tests are based on statistical probability. When one is dealing with groups, the use of statistics is certainly justified, since they have been developed from and for groups. An individual is justified in not locating his or her plant in an area where statistical studies show the average productivity is low. While there may be many good workers in the area, the owner's decision is concerned with the group and not with individuals.

In the hiring situation, we are dealing with individuals and not with groups; statistical data must be put aside while we investigate the individual. The fact that sixty percent of the people in a given group suffer from eye strain does not tell one anything about the individual before one. As a result, an individual would be unjust in attributing to a person the statistical characteristics of the group to which he or she belongs. Something similar may be said when we are dealing not with careful, scientific studies but with our own ideas about groups. Perhaps sixty percent of the teen-agers one knows personally are extroverts, but even if one's impression is correct, it does not tell one anything about this particular teen-ager. Individuals are always to be treated as individuals.

AFFIRMATIVE ACTION AND PREFERENTIAL HIRING

The term affirmative action is ambiguous since it has been used to designate three different actions. First, it can mean taking positive steps to recruit from minority or underprivileged groups. Second, it can mean that *all other things being equal,* the minority group member will be hired or promoted. Third, it can mean that even when *all things relevant to the job are not equal,* the minority group member will be given the job. In this third sense, affirmative action is equivalent to preferential hiring. It is important to stress the fact that the two are not identical in all cases.

Affirmative action in the first sense involves positive and therefore affirmative steps to reduce or eliminate the chance that qualified candidates are being kept from applying for a job or promotion. The steps in question may involve communicating job openings more widely in all schools and media, especially those used by groups which have historically been discriminated against. In other cases, the affirmative action involves encouraging women and minorities to take company training that will qualify them for promotion. Such actions are clearly ethical since they do not involve preferential treatment but rather creative extensions of job opportunities.

Affirmative action in the second sense, in which applicants are equal as regards job qualifications, is basically a method of resolving a tie. Unlike other methods such as tossing a coin, it has good social effects to recommend it. It is difficult, then, to see any serious ethical problem here.

The third meaning of affirmative action, which is equivalent to preferential hiring and reverse discrimination, poses real ethical problems. Despite all sorts of subtle distinctions, two sorts of justification are given for such preferential hiring. The one argument rests on the idea of restitution; the other rests on that of national survival in a crisis.

The restitution argument argues that the firm, or at least the firm as a designee of society, has an obligation to make restitution or reparation of the sins of the past against women and minority groups. While this argument has a plausible ring, there are basic objections to it.

In the first place, it is difficult to see the justice of making a living individual responsible for past injustices committed by a possibly unrelated individual. The sins of my grandfather against an individual do not put me in debt to the grandson of the offended individual unless it can be shown that I am unjustly in possession of his property. In the second place, while society certainly has an obligation to repair the damage done by society in the past, the restitutions should be based on need rather than on such factors as color or sex which have only an accidental connection with need.

Finally, if it is wrong to exclude a person because that person is a Black, it is equally wrong to exclude him or her because he or she is not a Black. Furthermore, most of our civil rights legislation, especially on the state level, would appear to forbid such practices. Not only ethics and law, but good business forbids preferential hiring. Much of the opposition to integration and fair employment practices springs from the fear that hiring Blacks will reduce the number of jobs available to other races. Preferential hiring serves to increase those fears by providing an objective basis for the anxiety. This can only make it more difficult to integrate work forces at the same time that it weakens morale.

Despite strong objections to the restitution argument for reverse discrimination or preferential hiring, there may be reasons of social necessity that could permit, or perhaps even tolerate, such practices for a time. When past and present injustices have created great social unrest, and even the more or less immediate threat of revolution, the social good can justify special sacrifices from citizens and special efforts from corporations. When race riots and riot related arson were tearing apart American cities during the sixties, the social order was threatened. Police action was not going to cure or alleviate the problem. In this emergency situation, then, broader social action was called for. Even policies involving reverse discrimination were temporarily justified in the name of the common good. In short, a national emergency can justify some temporary abridgment of the right to equal treatment. Preferential treatment, however, is not an inherent right, nor is the emergency justification of reverse discrimination automatic. The facts determine whether radical social intervention is necessary to preserve the social order.

NEPOTISM

Nepotism is potentially a case of preferential hiring. It may, however, have a legitimate place in the family firm where the hiring looks not only to efficiency, but to providing jobs for relatives. In these cases, the preference can be justified to a certain extent by the peculiar purpose of the firm. In all other cases, nepotism is unethical only if it involves real favoritism or discrimination.

Business people are concerned with the qualifications and impact of the relative. Assuming that the relative has qualifications at least roughly equal to other candidates, the decision should be based on a realistic evaluation of the effect of this hiring on the firm. The business person must ask questions like the following: Would hiring this person create jealousy and resentment? Will it discourage qualified outsiders from seeking work with the company? Will it create problems in firing and demoting? Will it inhibit the relative's development? Will it cause problems inside the family? It should be remembered than, in itself, being a relative is neither a virtue nor a vice. Ethically then, decisions should be made with consideration for the potential impact of the hiring decision as well as for the candidate's qualifications.

SPECIAL PROBLEMS

In theory, fair employment practices should pose no problems to the capable business person. In practice, he or she may face real difficulties. Hiring hall procedures by unions which do not obey the law, discrimination by employment agencies, moral and economic pressures from friends, associates, and customers may entangle the business person. While we cannot discuss all of these problems in detail, the following points should be kept in mind. If the employer has no intention of discriminating and is not covered by the law, the employer may often have a proportionate reason for temporarily cooperating with those who discriminate. Fear and timidity, however, are not permanent excuses. Indeed, the very difficulties which create a temporary excuse give rise to an obligation to remedy the factors which create the problem. In the concrete, this may mean working for the passage of laws that will enable men of good will to do the right thing without undue hardship. In other cases, it may involve cooperation with community groups attempting to eliminate prejudice. When possible, it will involve circumventing unions, hiring halls, and employment agencies which do discriminate.

We must stress the fact that, since many problems cannot be solved by isolated individuals or by business persons alone, there is an obligation to enter into broader forms of social cooperation. Ending discrimination in hiring helps to equalize opportunity, but it does not do away with the unnatural inequalities arising from poor education and poor family background. This residual but huge inequality is not solely or specially the problem of business, but it cannot be solved without the help of business. Therefore, business must at least support, if not initiate, programs designed to attack the root problems.

PROMOTIONS

The same principles apply to both hiring and promotions. In brief, job qualifications should dominate all decisions in the vast majority of cases. Unfortunately, the existence of demands for the recognition of seniority complicates this question.

Seniority *of itself* is no index of competence. It is not even an index of loyalty, since it may result from laziness or cowardice. In the abstract, then, seniority has no bearing on a decision to promote. In the concrete, seniority may indicate real job qualifications as well as length of service. Moreover, the expectations of workers, whether reasonable or not, may change the significance of seniority.[2] If workers expect seniority to count, management's disregard of their opinion may injure morale. On the other hand, if too much attention is given to mere years of service, management may discourage real initiative and lose talented young workers and executives.

Similar problems beset the manager who must decide whether to promote from within or to go outside the company. In the abstract, the manager should look only to competence. In the concrete, he or she must consider the impact of this decision on the employees, whether or not their attitudes are unreasonable. Here, as elsewhere, the existence of carefully written and fully promulgated policies can do much to control expectations and make sound ethical and business decisions easier to execute.

Some of the most difficult problems arise when a person has been promoted to a job which they cannot handle or which will seriously harm their health. Demoting such an individual not only involves wounding their pride and reducing their income but also makes a public admission of management failure. On the other hand, if the situation is allowed to continue, the individual's assistants and the company will suffer harm.

Generally such problems are unpleasant to meet head on. As a result, management attempts to evolve ingenious compromises. Sometimes, the individual is given an assistant or moved horizontally to a job they can handle. Sometimes job assignments are changed so that the work load or type of work

[2]Philip Selznick and Howard Vollmer, *Rule of Law in Industry: Seniority Rights* (Berkeley, California: Institute of Industrial Relations, 1962), suggests that these expectations may not be what they appear to be.

is different. Such maneuvers are possible in large or very profitable companies but may be too expensive in others. In these circumstances, it is generally necessary to seek a tactful method of demotion, which frequently turns out to be better for the man involved than for all others.

Nearly all our remarks on special problems and promotions indicate that the primacy of job qualifications is not absolute. A company is composed of people, not cyphers, so that the principle has to be adjusted to the concrete possibilities. What must be avoided is the arbitrary disregard of principle or the acceptance of unjust situations as immutable.

FIRING

In the absence of an explicit work contract, it was formerly assumed that both employer and employee had a right to terminate their agreement at will. Some individuals still assume this to be true. Quite aside from legal provisions, however, there are implicit contracts that limit or modify the right of both employer and employee. In many countries, these modifications have become the subject of law. In the United States, they are often stated in collective bargaining agreements and in labor law. While most American courts still adhere to the idea of employment at will when there is no contract, case law does recognize that some dismissals may be contrary to public policy or violate an implied duty of fair dealing. It should be noted that the courts have also discovered implied contracts in a company's personnel manual. Such extensions of the law appear to be consonant with, if not demanded by, sound business ethics. No matter what the law, we must still consider the basic ethics of firing.

Regardless of explicit contractual provisions, both employer and employee have obligations to each other which arise first from their common humanity and secondly from the definite social situation in which their agreement was made. This means that each side must take into consideration the legitimate interests and expectations of the other. While such interests may not always be decisive, they must be considered lest one be indifferent to the good of another human being.

Employers' obligations fall under the following three headings:

1. They must dismiss only for just cause.
2. They must observe due process.
3. They must seek to mitigate the harmful effects of dismissal, due attention being given to proportionality.

JUST CAUSE

Although the phrase "just cause" is necessarily vague, it certainly includes only factors pertinent to the running of a business. Thus, the whim of the employer, his or her personal political convictions, and the annoying mannerisms of an employee are not just causes for dismissal. Just causes will include mechanization, reduction in output, violation of discipline including conduct harmful to other workers, negligence, frequent illness, and prolonged absenteeism which is harmful to either the business or other workers.

It should be noted that an employer not only may dismiss for such just causes, but often *must* do so. While our emotions may balk at dismissing a poor employee who has a large number of children, this act may be necessary to protect the company and/or other workers. The lazy worker, for example, not only robs the business of the purchased services, but demoralizes others, and reduces overall efficiency. The dishonest worker harms the firm, not only by his or her own thefts but by inducing others to follow this example. For these reasons, sentiment must give way to an objective evaluation of the situation.

In many cases, sentiment harms the firm as well as the worker who should be fired. Tacit consent to inefficiency, laziness, or dishonesty only reinforces bad habits and makes it harder and harder to reform. Moreover, tacit consent can fill in the details in the work contract and set up false but powerful expectations that render dismissal progressively more difficult.

Since length of service changes the relationship, and so the implicit contract, the reason for dismissal must be more serious in the case of a veteran employee than in the case of an apprentice. There are several reasons for this. The efficiency of a business depends, in the vast majority of cases, on the stability of its work force. As a result, anything which disturbs confidence in the employer's recognition of service is liable to have harmful effects on both morale and recruiting. Simple common sense then would indicate that the reason for dismissal must offset this risk. In addition, senior employees have often sacrificed opportunities in order to stay with a company.

Carefully drawn up company policy can help to remove arbitrariness and reduce dissatisfaction. Some companies, for example, will not dismiss a worker over fifty, who has been with them at least twenty years, except for the grossest negligence or incapacity. Others provide for shifting burdens from older workers and putting them where they can pass on experience even though they may not be able to meet full job requirements.

DUE PROCESS

Due process safeguards not only the rights of the employee but the morale of other workers. It is not enough to be just. One must also appear just if the potentially harmful effects of dismissal are to be mitigated. Due process gives the assurance that decisions are not made arbitrarily and thus reinforces the confidence of the work force. Furthermore, because due process involves a system of checks and balances, it increases the objectivity of decisions.

The need for objectivity should be apparent. For many employers, dismissals are a highly emotional subject. All too often, employers are so concerned with a small set of factors that they lose the overall view necessary for making decisions that are ethically and economically sound. For example, the fact that an incapable employee has a large family and long years of service does not generally offset such evils as demoralization of the work force and serious inefficiency. To put it another way, the employer must remember that he or she has an obligation to protect all of the workers, and the interest of customers and owners. As a result, the employer needs some method of assuring adequate consideration of all of the factors involved. Ethically employers should always use the sanctions that cause the least harm, but they should not lose sight of the fact that, when warnings have been given, firing may be the only means left.

The exact process to be used cannot be determined in the abstract. Elaborate measures will be both unnecessary and too costly for the small firm, while overly simple procedures may be useless in a large one. In general, however, a workable procedure will be the result of an agreement arrived at by management and employees.

No matter what the details of the process the following would seem to constitute the minimum requirements:

1. The charge, that is the alleged just cause, must be clearly stated and supported with evidence.
2. The employee must have an opportunity to face his or her accuser, to refute the charge and to rebut the evidence.
3. There must be some provision for an appeal so that the final decisions are made by someone who is not directly involved with the employee in question.

The clear charge presumes that there were clear rules and/or clear expectations that had been carefully communicated to the employee beforehand. Vague labels such as "disloyalty" may be clear to the employer but truly obscure to the employee. In the absence of communication, there can be vast differences in expectation between managers and employees. Thus, such statements as, "They should have known," are no substitute for clear and effective communication of all rules and expectations.

The opportunity to confront, refute, and rebut is simple fairness. Just as there are six sides to every packing crate, there are at least two sides to every dispute. Thus, this step in the process helps to explore half truths, biases, personal pique, and conflicts of interest that may be behind a charge. After all, not all supervisors are automatically right.

MITIGATION OF HARMFUL EFFECTS

Even though an employer is justified in firing a worker, the employer must seek to mitigate the harmful effects of dismissal. Although a person may have a proportionate reason for risking or permitting the harmful effects of a dismissal, that person still has the basic obligation of using reasonable means to minimize the harm. This is recognized by ethical employers as well as by the law in many countries. In the United States, moreover, we have devised public means of lessening the effects of dismissal. The Unemployment Compensation Law is the principal example. However, since unemployment benefits are in many cases very meager, the employer may still have personal obligations.

Giving adequate notice of dismissal is one of the easier and more obvious methods of mitigating impacts. It costs the employer little and permits the employee to look for other work. Furthermore, it provides for some period of delay during which appeals can be made. It is difficult to determine the proper length of time of the notice period, but it would seem to be prudent for this to be stated explicitly in the work contract. Formal policy in these cases, as in so many others, regularizes expectations and so reinforces confidence in the fairness of the employer.

The obligation to mitigate harmful effects can be particularly serious in cases of plant relocation and major layoffs. The reason is simply that in these cases not only the workers and their families, but tradespeople, and, in some cases, entire communities may be affected. While it is impossible to specify which means of mitigation are to be used in a given case, there are many available. Adequate notice, retraining, and relocation of workers are possible procedures that may lessen harmful effects.

It should be recognized that in some cases the need for massive layoffs results from management's failure to do its job or from its refusal to find means of removing the underlying causes. For example, many businesses are highly seasonal, not because this is absolutely necessary, but because the employers have accepted a given situation as natural. Since it is good business as well as good ethics to iron out seasonal fluctuations, management should not overlook obligations in this area. Quite frequently the causes of seasonal variation can only be attacked by broad economic cooperation among business, government, and labor. While such cooperation may be foreign to the mentality of many business people, the fact remains that it can be necessary and therefore obligatory.

THE OBLIGATIONS OF EMPLOYEES

Although most obligations of the employee will be treated in Chapters Six, Seven, and Eight, it should be noted that the implicit contract of employment binds both parties. Like the employer, the employee must make decisions with consideration for the welfare of the company and of fellow workers. He or she may be free to quit at the end of a formal contract, but fair dealing requires that adequate notice be given in most cases. Indeed, unless there is a grounded fear of unjust retaliation, fairness would generally demand that employers be given a chance to match offers and to remedy causes of dissatisfaction. After all, the management, too, has its reasonably founded expectations.

SOME POINTS OF BROADER SIGNIFICANCE

In the previous pages we have had occasion to mention two points, which will appear so frequently that they deserve to be underlined and explained lest their significance escape the reader. First, *carefully worked-out policies can prevent many problems.* Second, *in many areas a policy should be the result of bilateral agreements if it is to be truly fair.*

A careful policy not only regularizes expectations but gives some assurance that decisions will not be made in an arbitrary manner. Good business alone would seem to demand such policy. Frequently, people confuse policy with detailed rule making and avoid the task, since they think the situation too complex. Often, avoidance of the task actually results from the inability to deal with a problem or the unwillingness to limit the arbitrary. While there is some justification for moving slowly when the situation is complicated, a lack of executive talent and an insecure personality is betrayed by the failure to face problems and make commitments. These two characteristics, plus the absence of policy, can only breed ethical problems and cause worker dissatisfaction. Although many people will not recognize such attitudes as moral defects, experience shows that they generate as much unethical conduct as does downright dishonesty.

Our insistence on the need for bilateral agreements runs counter to the idea that management's rights extend to everything that is not explicitly denied them by law or contract. While we do not intend to deny that management has and must have spheres of independent judgment, it should be recognized that people are rightfully less and less willing to enter into work contracts where one party lays down all conditions and reserves the right to interpret the contract. Resentment of such situations has promoted unionism and collective bargaining. While all problems may not be solved by collective agreements, since these too can be effected by power rather than by reasoned discourse, there is much to recommend them. Among other things, people feel a greater obligation to abide by free agreements with the result that truly free contracts assure greater cohesion and cooperation. Workers can be attached strongly even to poor programs and procedures if they are their own.

The reason for demanding bilateral agreements in many areas is not economic but ethical. The mere ownership of property or the control of it does not bestow complete authority over the workers who handle the property, nor does the power to exact consent to working conditions constitute a legitimate right to extort them. Furthermore there are areas where management may not even be competent to make the decisions. While it is not the function of an introductory book to explore all these questions in depth, students of business must realize that such questions must be considered before business can solve many of its ethical and economic problems.

BY WAY OF SUMMARY

With the exception of some family firms, business should hire, fire, and promote on the basis of a person's actual or potential contribution to the firm. To put it another way, the job relevance of a worker's skills should be the only factor considered in nonfamily firms. Even temporary exceptions need to be justified by some overriding social good. In the case of firings, however, not only just (job-relevant) causes but due process must be present. Finally, as always, harmful consequences should be mitigated whenever possible.

4

WAGES AND WORKING CONDITIONS

INTRODUCTION

The ethics of hiring, firing, and promotions are largely a question of equal treatment of persons having equal job qualifications. The ethics of wages and working conditions are not so simple. They involve not only job qualifications, but the worker's human needs, and the functioning of the economy as a whole. Because so many factors enter into the ethical judgment of the fairness of wages and the decency of working conditions, many thinkers despair of establishing any principles. Granted that there are few fixed guide lines, we still need some frame of reference lest management and labor settle disputes on the basis of power rather than in terms of at least minimal justice.

WAGES VERSUS INCOME

Most discussions of the fair wage start with the assumption that wages are or ought to be the principal if not the only source of a worker's income. This leads to the conclusion that the fair wage ought to be sufficient to permit workers and their families to live in decent comfort according to the increasing standards of society. This comfort includes the possibility of making some provision for sickness and old age as well as for the education of children.

In an ideal world, the fair wage would certainly measure up to the minimum described above. In the real world, even in the very wealthy real world of the American economy, the ideal faces great obstacles. For business persons, wages are a cost to be kept down or at best an incentive used to increase production. If they add proper differentials to the ideal minimum, they will often have to price themselves out of the market or replace workers with machines. Even if the ideal minimum *wage* is possible in some cases, it may not supply a decent minimum *income* for long. The worker may manage his or her money poorly and fail to make provision for sickness and old age. Inflation may rob wages of their purchasing power and raise the minimum level of money income necessary for decent comfort.

These facts lead to two conclusions. First, *income* rather than *wages* is the significant concept. Secondly, an adequate income cannot be supplied without broad social cooperation and some political control. As a result, the problem and the ideal are only partially the responsibility of business. Although this has not been completely accepted in theory, it has been recognized in practice. Social Security, Unemployment Compensation, compulsory accident insurance, medical assistance to the aged, public education, free lunch programs for children, the negative income tax, low income allowances and supplemental unemployment benefits as well as the ever increasing package of fringes supplied by business itself are all signs that the American society recognizes that income rather than wages is the significant reality. In some nations there are family allowances for children, free health care for everyone, and also sorts of subsidized housing. All of these aim at providing some sort of decent minimum income for everyone. The fact that no society has succeeded completely merely points to the inherent limitations of mankind no matter how great its good intentions.

FAIR WAGES

In view of all this, the fairness of wages cannot, in practice, be established solely in terms of the needs of workers and their families. This does not mean, however, that wages are to be determined exclusively in terms of the market for labor or of the contribution of workers to the company. The market for labor can be manipulated in a variety of ways, and it is almost impossible to measure the actual contributions of workers. Demand, supply, and contribution do enter into the question, but they do not establish a complete norm of fairness.

In the opinion of the present writers, there is no *a priori* way of determining what constitutes a just wage or salary. Anyone familiar with the maze of wage and salary administration will agree. Wages must be related to the contribution to the firm, to the market for both labor and products, to the competitive position of the company, and to the power of the unions as well as to the needs of workers and their families. If any of these factors is ignored, grave harm may result, no matter how good the intentions of management. All of these factors establish demands and limiting conditions. They create a framework of concrete and limited possibilities within which justice is to be found.

Since we have not worked out any satisfactory mathematical formula which will determine the proper weight to be given to all factors in all circumstances, it seems that a fair wage, as distinguished from a fair income, can be determined only by a fair work contract. A fair work contract will generally depend on the existence of *free and fair negotiations* which respect the positions of all parties involved. This is a big order, since in many cases consumers and society at large have a very big stake in wage negotiations. The concept, however, is sound, even though we have not evolved a social mechanism for taking care of the interests of third parties.

A contract is truly fair when both sides are free and conscious of the implications of their acts. Freedom does not imply that the contracting parties are overjoyed but that their agreement is reasonable. The agreement is not reasonable, and there is no true freedom if one or both sides have used fraud, power, passion, or ignorance to bring about an agreement that would have been otherwise rejected. To be sure, the impairment of freedom must be substantial to vitiate a contract and make it truly unfair, but it can occur. Starving workers will agree to almost anything to keep their children alive. A company that cannot afford a strike may have to submit to demands short of those that will cause immediate bankruptcy. In short, power can be substituted for reason and destroy even the minimal freedom needed for a fair contract. In our economy, where large companies and large unions are mingled with small companies, small unions, and no unions at all, the possibility of unfairness in a substantial degree is all too great.

Since we have no really adequate social means of assuring even approximate equality and freedom between all bargaining agents, fair agreements may often be accidents or exceptions rather than the rule. Indeed, because we are dealing with people, we need special efforts on the part of employers, workers, and unions, and some social control which affects the areas untouched by organized labor or vitiated by power imbalances. As already noted, the shifting power positions of companies and unions may also make it necessary to provide institutions which allow consumers and other vitally interested parties to be represented.

While the ultimate solution to the problem of fair wages still lies in the future, in practice employers can at least check their wages against the following points:

1. The going *wage* in an industry and area when this is publicly accepted as "just"
2. The adequacy of the worker's *income* in terms of minimum standards such as those set by the Department of Labor
3. The concrete possibility of helping the worker to a more adequate income

The going wage in an industry and area which is publicly accepted as "just" supplies a rough norm of fairness unless it has been set largely as a result of power, fraud, passion, or ignorance. If an employer is paying substantially below this going wage for a given job in an area, he or she ought to question the fairness of his wage contract. Similarly, if employers have agreed to keep wages low and succeed because labor is poorly organized, the fairness of the contract is questionable.

While the going wage can provide a rough rule of thumb, it is not a final norm. The aim of society is still an income that will provide security and a decent living. If the going wage and other sources of income still leave large groups of employees below the minimum level, the business person must do his or her share in helping society to provide all with a minimum decent income.

Business people have two responsibilities in this area. First, they should cooperate with other groups in raising the social sources of income. Such sources of income are, for example, public education, public health services, and recreational facilities, all of which represent economic benefits. Second, they should strive to make their businesses so efficient that they can raise the going rates to a point where they and other sources of income are adequate for decent living. This means that although the contractual wage may be fair in one sense, the business person as a citizen and manager has obligations beyond the minimum of the contract. These are shared obligations and limited ones, but they do exist.

Actually the worst offenders against the obligations just mentioned are schools and hospitals, which not only pay low wages but make little effort to raise them. Some businesses offend by moving to areas where they exploit cheap labor and beat down those who want to bargain as equals. While owners, stockholders, and consumers may have claims on a business, the demands of workers cannot and should not be ignored. Consumers must pay the true cost of what they buy. Stockholders must realize that as a general rule wages are closer to the necessities of life than dividends.

Some will object that the approach to the wage situation is too idealistic and that the accepted treatment is too favorable to employers because the practical norms, as opposed to the ideal ones, tend to justify the *status quo*. Both criticisms are fair and to the point. In defense it can only be said that there appears to be no other realistic solution except one that develops from an attainable minimum and moves toward an obligatory ideal.

PROFIT SHARING

The increased number of firms engaged in profit sharing raises the question of whether or not employees have a right to share in profits. The answer depends on one's definition of profits. However, no matter how profits are defined, it is generally held that when the employee is receiving a fair wage, he or she is not entitled to any additional money as a matter of strict right. The reason is simply that the employee has freely agreed to limit his or her claims in justice to the agreed wage. He or she may, of course, seek to change the wage contract in order to obtain a share of profits provided, of course, that power or fraud is not used. The employer is morally free to grant a new contract or not, so long as he or she is paying a just wage.

The theory stated above is certainly applicable to the vast majority of companies. However, there appears to be a new situation developing in which workers may have a claim to some share in the profits in addition to their contractual provisions. In the case of the company which no one owns in any real sense (although the stockholders may hold legal title of some sort), contribution rather than contract may be the only realistic title to income. In such companies, workers may, because of their contribution and cooperation within a sort of open contract, have a claim to share in the surplus to the extent that they have contributed to it. As yet, thinking has not advanced far enough to make this type of claim very precise. However, the student should anticipate its occurrence.

STABILITY OF WORK

Insecurity in employment has been one of the major factors leading to unionization. The reason is simply that human beings fear insecurity as much as they fear poverty. This is a reasonable fear since persons cannot order their own life or provide for the future if they are in doubt as to the security of their work and income. Although union negotiations and unemployment compensation have done much to mitigate the evils of insecurity, the problem will become more acute. Automation, the growth of seasonal industries, and plant relocations threaten security.

Although stable production would be in their own best interests, employers have resigned themselves to periodic layoffs and seasonal variations as a fact of economic life. However, the obligation to run a business efficiently and to avoid harmful consequences for others creates an obligation to work for the stabilization of production and employment. Realistically, such stability often depends on factors beyond the direct control of the individual employer. Industry custom, technological advances, and the general state of the economy often dictate the level of production at a given time. These facts do not excuse the employer from his or her obligation but transform it into a duty to work with others in producing an overall pattern of stability.

Concretely, employers must cooperate in planning on a broader social level. Planning may be a dirty word for many, but it is only asking business people to concede to society the rational approach of employers within their firms. Some may object that planning involves a loss of freedom. This is a debatable question. The real concern is whether or not planning would be beneficial in the advancement of human well-being and freedom.

Later in this book we shall return to these questions, but even at the beginning it is important to realize that there are problems in business ethics that cannot be solved without broad social cooperation in industry and in the economy as a whole. Too often business ethics has been studied as if it had no social dimension and as if business people could bring about social justice on their own. Unless the total social and economic system is examined, we shall have only excuses and no solutions to even such a fundamental problem as that of wages.

WORKING CONDITIONS

The American experience with labor relations indicates that working conditions are as significant an area as wages and work stability. Despite this, it is all too easy to overlook the ethical problems by accepting—as right and just—situations that exist and always have existed. Legislation and conscience have solved many problems. We should not forget, however, that in the past, mine donkeys were better cared for than miners. Even today there are cases where migrant workers are housed like animals with little or no consideration given to the health and education of their children.

A worker should not be treated as a thing. Neither should the worker or his or her family be exposed to physical, psychological, or moral harm without a proportionate reason. To disregard safety in these areas is to disregard the good of a human being and even the simplest ethical principles. There are cases where nothing can be done to eliminate risks or where the cost of eliminating them may be prohibitive, but the general principle stands: safety is ethically important.

While cases involving physical harm would seem to be obvious, scientific research has shown that not all dangers are obvious and that some dangers are far more widespread than anyone realized in the past. The hidden dangers come from exposure to chemicals or other substances that have their full effect only after long periods of time or as the result of cumulative exposure. Thus the Occupational Safety and Health Act (OSHA) seeks to impose obligations that go well beyond those of traditional ethics. Thus in promulgating standards for toxic materials the Act wants a norm that "most adequately assures, to the extent feasible, on the basis of the best available evidence, that no employee will suffer material impairment of health or functional capacity even if such employee has regular exposure to the hazard dealt with. . . for the period of his or her working life." Here there is no question of reasonable efforts but of an all out effort within the limits of "feasibility."

Such rigorous standards have led to many disputes. Without attempting to settle those disputes, we would like to stress a factor that must not be overlooked. First, the costs of industrial accidents and industrially caused health problems are high. Society pays much of those costs despite worker's compensation. The law, then, seeks to shift those costs from society to the companies that are involved and so to the customers who buy from that company. As we shall see in Chapter Nine, something similar is going on with regard to consumer product safety.

Although inclined to approve of rigorous regulation of factors relating to worker safety, we do not want to approve of enforcement measures that amount to harassment or trial without due process. Even the most noble purpose does not justify stupidity and injustice.

Working conditions can affect not only physical safety but also the ethics and human dignity of the workers. While some people minimize the importance of these areas, both deserve consideration.

Poor cash and inventory control systems can tempt workers to steal. Therefore, both good ethics and good business require that reasonable measures be taken for the protection of the worker and the firm. Similarly, new workers should be warned of the ethical pitfalls connected with their jobs and be assured of the firm's stand on principles. This might seem naive, but many new employees are corrupted by being involved in bribery or theft before they know what is happening. Also, the office clique may fill the vacuum left by management and establish its own policies, which may harm both company and worker.

Managers and supervisors might also keep their eyes open for more serious schemes that exploit the gullible in their employ. There are individuals who use a place of business to sell tickets for fraudulent lotteries. There are scoundrels who coerce the timid into cooperating in all sorts of unethical practices under the threat of false denunciation and subsequent dismissal. While there are no statistics on the frequency of such occurrences, our own consulting work indicates that these situations are not rarities.

Blackmail on the job is frequently coupled with sexual harassment which covers everything from obscene remarks to extorted intercourse with all sorts of unwanted touches, attentions, and advances in between. Today such activities are not only unethical but forbidden by law. As a result, employers and supervisors have a legal obligation to discourage and even to prevent sexual harassment of workers. While some want to make this an issue of the women's liberation movement, male employees have also been harassed in these ways. In any event, it is a matter of human dignity and not of political movements alone.

The boss is not an almighty overseer who can or should control the private morals of his or her employees, but he or she certainly cannot be indifferent to what goes on in the firm. If the boss recalls the confusion and loneliness of his or her own first weeks at work, he or she may realize that young workers need advice, help, and protection. A person in such a position should be aware that the type of situation we have been describing is not conducive to a high level of morale and efficiency. If such a person fails to act, he or she gives tacit approval to favoritism, office politics, featherbedding, and conspiracy in theft.

Managers on all levels should remember that their power to command, reward, and punish is not self-justifying. It carries with it a responsibility to use power for the good of the company, with due respect for the rights and consciences of others. Forcing, ordering, or encouraging employees to act unethically, or to cooperate in unethical activities, is doubly wrong, for the manager who does this should remember that he or she has not only harmed another human being but has taught that person that the manager is not worthy of trust.

Working conditions can affect both the home life and family finances. While an employer is not directly responsible for such effects in the vast majority of cases, he or she should consider them and the offsetting goods. The person who is constantly on the road will have grave difficulty in fulfilling his or her duties as a parent or spouse. Although travel is a part of the employee's job, the ethical employer will ask if all the travel is necessary in view of the effects on the spouse and children.

Job transfers can involve considerable expense and even increased living costs. While the employer can often force the worker to pay these, conscientious firms will make appropriate allowances for both transportation and cost of living adjustments. This is a question of fairness and of good internal relations.

The list of situations involving detrimental effects on workers and their families is almost endless. A complete catalogue, however, can say no more than that the results should be considered, since a person is not a thing but a human being with his or her own rights and dignity.

WORK SATISFACTION

Studies have shown that although good wages may keep people from complaining, they do not motivate workers as successfully as work satisfaction. For this reason, employers have an economic interest in work satisfaction. There are, however, deeper human considerations involved. Work occupies a large part of a person's day. Unless the job is humanly satisfying, not only their productivity but their whole life is diminished. Humans need to find significance in what they do. Unconsciously, at least, they need to feel that they have created something, served others, and left their mark upon the world. Work should provide the opportunity for this sense of fulfillment.

Since both employers and employees have an important stake in work satisfaction, there is certainly an obligation to consider this aspect of business. Lack of imagination and initiative can contribute to moral failures as well as business losses. While it is difficult to be more specific, it would certainly appear that the business person has a real obligation to study and utilize the vast literature concerned with motivation.

Unless this very human side of business is appreciated and studied, the executive may discover that highly efficient technological innovations have been frustrated by unhappy human beings whose sense of justice has been offended. It will also be clear to the knowledgeable reader that both the obligation to respect workers and the obligation to run an efficient firm can be fulfilled only by the truly competent manager who has both technical skill and human sensitivity. The study of managerial and industrial psychology is ethically imperative, but human sensitivity will not result from mere textbook knowledge. The first-class managers must also know themselves, their own fears, limitations, and values if they are to respect others and compensate for their own deficiencies. Only in this way can they be sure that their perception of the needs and rights of others has not been distorted by selfishness and by a narrow view of the function of management.

BY WAY OF SUMMARY

While the fairness of wages is largely a question of free agreement and custom, business has an obligation to cooperate with government and labor in increasing the social sources of income so that people can have a decent life. Similar cooperation should aim at stabilizing employment. Although there is room for dispute about the soundness of OSHA regulations, worker safety should be a major concern for management. Finally, managers should be aware that their decisions affect employees in many ways. They must, of course, be especially sensitive and responsive to the harmful effects of managerial decisions.

5

PRIVATE LIVES AND COMPANY LIVES

INTRODUCTION

In the days of the company town, everyone knew where he stood even if he did not like it. The company controlled the plant, the stores, the credit, the real estate, and the political machine. If someone was dissatisfied, he could move out of town. This situation has changed for the better in America, but similar problems still exist.

1. Does a firm have a right to demand that workers contribute to the Community Chest?
2. Does a firm have a right to force employees into civic activities?
3. Can a firm ethically limit the political activity of employees?
4. Is it ethical to impose personality and lie detector tests and to "bug" the rest room?

All of these questions center on the problem of privacy. They all involve ethical problems concerned with the company's right to limit the freedom of the employee off the job; to interfere directly or indirectly with the private life of the employee, and to violate the psychic, physical or social privacy of the individual on or off the job.

RISE OF THE PROBLEM

The old-style paternalist had no doubts about his rights since he assumed that everything was his business and that his workers were his children. While this view was accepted by workers, there was no protest and, therefore, little consideration of the problem. Similarly, the man who viewed his workers as so many hands to produce physical labor had few worries about his rights. He simply fired persons when they did not produce and replaced them with others.

The problem is acute when the manager realizes that productivity is controlled by more than muscle and that the company reputation is an important source of profits. The new manager generally realizes that he or she is not the head of a family, but research has shown that many aspects of a worker's life and personality do influence the good of the company. The manager who works on the United Way appeal in the community may reflect favorably on the company just as an employee who is a member of a terroristic motorcycle gang may damage the firm's public image. As a result of such influences on the company, managers have become more and more interested in those areas that ordinarily should be considered private. At this point, the temptation to interfere creates an ethical problem and raises questions about what are the areas of legitimate interest.

At the same time that managers became more interested in all aspects of the employee's life, sophisticated techniques made it possible to penetrate areas that once were more or less protected from easy investigation. Not only efficient credit checks and private investigating services but the lie detector, personality tests, and all sorts of electronic snooping devices raise questions about the ethicality of information gathering in a variety of employment contexts. Thus, there is a question not only of what may be legitimately investigated but of what means are ethical.

THE VALUE OF PRIVACY

The questions posed above are difficult to answer not only because they involve complicated situations but because many people see little or no value in privacy. We have become so accustomed to certain invasions of privacy that they are accepted as a matter of course. Yet privacy is an important value that can be manifested in three areas: the psychic, the physical, and the social.

The most basic and sacred privacy is psychic. It is the privacy of the inner sphere, of man's thoughts, ideals, ambitions, and feelings. It is the area of personality that is especially human and especially personal. Indeed, so intimate is the union between this sphere and the person that it is often impossible to distinguish them. While there are levels of privacy and therefore room for distinctions, the essential point should be clear: The psychic sphere belongs to human beings in a special way and demands special respect.

Individuals manifest their inner life in many ways. Gestures, handwriting, facial expressions, and language reveal edges of the psychic sphere. In addition, individuals may want to reveal other areas to those who can help them or to those whom they love. In general, however, most of us keep large areas concealed not only from the general public but even from those who are close

to us. There are good reasons for such secrecy. In the first place, it protects us from exploitation at the hands of those who might want to use us for their own purposes. In the second place, indiscriminate revelation of the inner sphere can disturb both the individual and those who receive his or her confidences. For these reasons, an individual has the right and often the obligation to protect his or her psychic privacy. Others have a corresponding obligation to respect this inner sphere.

By the very nature of the case, the rights to psychic privacy are not absolute. A person may be obliged to reveal their inner life to a psychologist if this is necessary for their own mental health. For good and sufficient reason, a person may choose to reveal him or herself to another. An employer may even have the right to ask for the revelation of some inner life if this is necessary for the protection of the individual, fellow workers, or the company. Such need, however, ought to be established rather than assumed.

Physical privacy is a necessary means to the protection of psychic privacy. Unless there are times and places where individuals can share their inner sphere with those they love or with those who will help them, they will be deprived of many necessary goods. Husband and wife, doctor and patient, lawyer and client, employer and employee—all need the protection of physical privacy if they are to do their jobs.

Some courts have decided that physical privacy is violated only by direct physical trespass. According to these, spying through binoculars or by means of microphones outside the owner's property is not a violation of the owner's privacy. This is a narrow and dangerous view, for modern techniques can cause the harm without direct physical trespass. A person's right to privacy is not bounded by his or her property lines. Actually, the right to privacy has nothing to do with property in the ordinary sense. It is rather a right concerned with the protection of feelings and personal relations and with the physical conditions necessary to their protection. For this reason, there can be a violation of physical privacy even when there is no legal trespass. Bugging phones or private lounges on company property certainly destroys the protection of feelings and personal relations. Even from a business point of view it is not good for a boss to know what his or her employees really think about the head person. Certainly, human relations in general would deteriorate if we all knew everything about one another. Physical privacy is a necessary means for permitting us to be ourselves and still maintain social and business relations with others.

The right to such privacy is not absolute, but law has recognized its existence. Even the police cannot search a person's home except in carefully delineated circumstances. We have laws against the "Peeping Tom." Our society has always condemned the nosy person because of the harm which ensues from idle snooping and gossiping. At the same time, we recognize that spying is legitimate in time of war, since the right of one group to privacy is limited by the right of the other group to protect itself against attack.

Not merely psychic and physical privacy, but social-role privacy is necessary for the individual and society. Each of us must play a number of roles if society is to function efficiently. Thus, an individual must be a father, a husband, a mother, a wife, a citizen, as well as an administrator if he or she is to fulfill all duties. Often this is impossible unless the roles are separated and insulated one from the other. For example, as a citizen one may be obliged to protest something that the business community favors. If roles cannot be separated, the political community may lose a valuable leader. So too, the manager of a firm does not want the fear of reprisals against the family to interfere with sound business judgment. While role distinctions cannot be maintained completely, the breakdown of barriers can cause very great harm. As a result, secrecy and privacy are needed as supports of role distinction.

At the very least, privacy is necessary in order to protect the individual from self-incrimination and from the destruction of his or her reputation. As a result, even when there are legitimate reasons for invading privacy, there is always an obligation to protect the individual as much as possible.

With these points in mind, we can return to the principal questions. What areas are of legitimate interest to the employer? What means of investigation are ethical in various circumstances?

AREAS OF LEGITIMATE INTEREST

A firm is legitimately interested in *whatever influences work performance in any significant way.* After all, the company does pay for the employee's work even though it cannot buy or lease the worker himself.

Heavy drinking, heavy gambling by a controller, and loose talk by key employees are pertinent to job performance, but a person's fidelity in marriage or membership in a nudist camp are not. There are in-between cases too, but the company should look to the significance of the relationship unless it involves itself in the gathering of all sorts of expensive data that have little bearing on the job. Very often even information about emotional stability or aspirations may have little predictive value, since it is difficult to say how a person will react in a specific situation and to specific co-workers. Tests developed for clinical use may help in weeding out obvious misfits, but they may give little information about positive job performance. There is need for considerable reserve unless an unfounded enthusiasm for tests causes companies to pry deeper than is their right. Furthermore, an interest in details beyond the truly significant can arouse hostility in workers who will rightly feel that the company is trying to run their entire lives. The fact that the interest is legitimate, however, does not mean that all means of gathering data are justified.

The more difficult problems arise in regard to dealing with private acts and information which affect the *company image.* The problem is particularly great since, as people mount the ladder of the company hierarchy, the influence of their activities on the company image are often significant for work performance. If a mill worker belongs to the Communist Party, the job performance is not affected, and the effect on the company image is probably negligible. If a vice-president belongs to the American Nazi Party, the situation is different, since people may not want to deal with him or with a company that has such a man in a key position. This could be true even if the executive does not identify his public acts with the company.

Even though a company may at times have a legitimate interest in private activities which affect the *image* and the workings of the company, this does not mean that it can ethically interfere with these activities. Company control of its employees' political activity may not be healthy for the nation and the community. It can slow down change and free debate, and favor the *status quo*. Furthermore, unless there is a clear policy and provision for due process, decisions may be arbitrary. To put it another way, the fact of citizenship in the firm should not deprive people of their rights to fair treatment and the right to participate in the general political life of the nation. Labor law protects workers in this area, but management people do not have the same benefits. Companies, then, should make sure that their interference is really necessary and not the result of emotionalism or short-sighted selfishness.

Often privacy is disregarded not in the comdemnation of outside activities but in the "encouragement" of civic participation which will improve executive skills and the company image and power. The aspiring young executive may be told—if not actually commanded—to run for the school board, head up the Community Chest drive, or become active in some worthwhile civic activity. Generally speaking, the community may benefit from this, but does the company have the right to bring real pressure to bear? Similarly, does a company have a right to force contributions to charity or political parties in the interest of the company reputation? Where does legitimate persuasion end and polite blackmail begin? Although each case will be highly individual, we would suggest that the following are sound guide lines.

In general, the assumption ought to be that the individual's right is primary and that there should not be unreasonable interference. The reasonableness of the interference, however, cannot be determined unilaterally, since self-interest blinds. This is to say that solid ethical norms in this area can only be established by a form of collective bargaining.

For many businesses, there is an additional problem. Modern business involves a great deal of traveling. The need for this is well understood by employees and accepted as a part of their working conditions. The word *need* must be stressed, for time spent away from home creates problems that can be justified only if the traveling is necessary. If the effects on spouse and children are completely disregarded, a company may be acting as if it owned not only the employee, but his or her family as well. Once again precise norms may be impossible, but there is certainly an obligation to consider the effects of travel on the private lives of employees.

GARNISHMENTS

Although many employers are not concerned about the problems we have mentioned above, there is considerable worry about the problem of garnishments. A garnishment involves the legal attachment of wages for payment of debts. It forces the company to act as a collection agency for some creditor who has issued a legal judgment against an employee. Most of the time, the existence of a garnishment will also indicate that the employee is a bad credit risk.

Some companies have a policy of firing an employee after the second garnishment. At first glance, this might seem like an unwarranted interference with private life. However, this is not the case when there is an explicit company policy. The company rightfully objects to its accounting costs being increased by the carelessness of employees. For this reason, the garnishment, though it may not pertain to job performance, certainly affects the good of the company and not merely its image.

THE MEANS OF INVESTIGATION

Although a company may have a legitimate interest in many of its employees' activities, not all means of investigation are ethical. Privacy, as noted previously, has its claims even though they are not absolute in ethics. In taking a job, the employee certainly surrenders part of his or her privacy. Individuals agree to *ordinary* supervision of their work and to *ordinary* investigation of their suitability for the position. The ethical problem is concerned with the often hazy line between the ordinary and reasonable and the extraordinary and unreasonable interference with privacy. In the concrete, what means are reasonable in what circumstances? Can a company use wire taps, hidden television, polygraph tests, and personality testing, or are these ruled out because they are not common and ordinary?

Here as in the previous pages, the benefit of the doubt belongs to the employee; the right to use less common methods of surveillance and investigation must be justified by a proportionate reason. We might ask, for example, if some less questionable action would suffice to protect the firm and the rights of honest workers. The manager might also ask him or herself if honest employees would freely cooperate if they knew what was at stake. The first question considers the necessity of the measure for the social good of the firm and the protection of a worker's more basic rights. The second question is concerned with whether or not the surveillance may be considered a reasonable part of the work contract itself.

If wiring a *work area* is necessary to prevent thefts that cannot be controlled by ordinary means, one would tend to think that the company had a proportionate reason. Wiring might be necessary when employees were handling small valuable items such as drugs or diamonds. Even in these cases, the existence of the wiring should be known to the workers so that they may protect their legitimate secrets. The use of spies or secret wiring in the work area or of *any devices in such non-work areas as lounges and rest rooms* would require far more serious reasons. These should be of the type required for the authorization of a search warrant; there should be the founded suspicion that the procedure will unearth evidence of a serious crime that has already occurred. The neurotic suspicion that something might be discovered or the desire to pick up a useful tid-bit do not constitute reasonable grounds for invading privacy.

Even when there are reasonable grounds for the use of the methods mentioned above, there remains an obligation to protect the workers from harmful side effects. There will be information about private lives and feelings collected in the big net, and these facts must be destroyed, forgotten, or disregarded, since the company has no right to collect and use such information. This may require considerable restraint if the boss discovers that his "admiring" secretary really thinks he is a fraud. Indeed, it is because the surveillance may turn up just this sort of information that grave reasons are needed to justify the risk.

The obligation to protect workers exists in other areas. It can be ethical to use lie detector tests in screening applicants for responsibilities such as handling controlled drugs and large sums of currency, but there is an obligation to hire a skilled polygraph operator and to interpret results with great caution. In addition, even valid results must either be destroyed or guarded so that their use is confined to those who really need the information for making decisions. We shall have more to say on this in Chapter Seven when we treat the obligation of secrecy.

The problem of personality testing has been treated at some length in *Ethics in Business.*[1] Here we wish only to recall some major conclusions with regard to interference with psychic privacy. As in the cases above, the invasion needs justification, since the right of the individual is primary. More extensive invasions require the free consent of the employee. All information must be interpreted only by competent people and used with reserve even when its use is necessary. Finally, results and data should be destroyed when the employee leaves the company and guarded carefully in the meantime.

TOWARD A SOLUTION

The right of the individual to privacy is primary and gives way only to the proven reasonableness of interference by either a company or society in general. In many cases privacy is necessary for the growth of the individual and the functioning of the group. Privacy permits us to enter into intimate relationships which would never occur in the public eye. It permits us to distinguish our roles and to keep separate those aspects of our lives that ought to be kept separate. The goods involved cannot be dismissed lightly. As a result, a company should ask itself if interference is *necessary* since it is obvious that it can often be useful.

[1]Thomas M. Garrett, *Ethics in Business* (New York: Sheed, 1963), pp. 97–109.

The use of force to interfere with privacy is a sure indication that injustice is involved except in those cases where an explicit and free contract has granted such authority to the employer. The use of blackmail, even in a good cause, is unethical. While it is difficult to distinguish between "reasonable persuasion" and "blackmail," the extreme cases are clear enough. The in-between cases can sometimes be settled by asking the question, "Would I resent this being done to me?" The best method, of course, is to seek the advice of an honest and uninvolved outsider.

Actually, the best way to handle the gray area of privacy is by means of collective bargaining that results in an explicit contract. In many cases this bargaining is ethically necessary, since neither side has the information required to make a founded judgment of what is reasonable. Only an agreement based on careful discussion can result in even an approximately just and workable norm. Existing practice in either a company or an industry is not necessarily a good norm, since it may have resulted from unilateral decisions forced on a group that had no means of redress.

To insure justice, the norms developed by collective bargaining must also be subject to some form of due process lest arbitrary and unilateral interpretations and enforcement undo the bilateral agreement. Some people may look at this as an infringement of management rights. They forget, however, that management does not have rights over the workers by virtue of property ownership but only through contract, or in some cases popular consent. The manager is not the family's parent, endowed by nature with authority over every aspect of employees' lives.

In the last analysis, contracts and collective bargaining may not be sufficient to guarantee due process and fair treatment. In the *Government of Corporations,* Richard Eells has noted the need for a bill of rights that will protect employees against the private government of the firm just as the Constitution protects citizens against the civil rulers.[2] It may be, then, that we will not even approximate true justice in business until we have established some form of corporation constitutionalism that provides both the rules of the game and some form of outside review.

BY WAY OF SUMMARY

While a company has a legitimate interest in employee activity that is directly job-relevant, the right to privacy (physical, psychic, and social) forbids intrusion in most areas as well as limits the means of investigation. Gray areas should be a matter of collective bargaining if not of corporate constitutionalism. While philosophers, public policy and management theorists can contribute to the debate, in the end the courts will probably make the operative decisions on these very complex privacy issues.

[2]Richard Eells, *The Government of Corporations* (New York: Free Press, 1962), p. 268. See also, David Ewing, *Freedom Inside the Organization,* (New York: E. P. Dutton Co., 1977).

6

FIDUCIARY RELATIONSHIPS AND CONFLICTS OF INTEREST

INTRODUCTION

The contract of employment creates obligations for the employee as well as for the employer. Basically, the employee is bound to give an honest day's work for an honest day's wages. While this is true, it is neither a perfectly clear nor an all-inclusive statement of the employee's obligations to the firm. The present chapter and the two which follow attempt to spell out some of the duties that can easily be overlooked. In particular, these chapters will look at those duties which are implicit rather than clearly stated.

By the work contract the employee agrees to give a more or less specified amount of time, energy, and intelligence to the firm in return for income. While the employee does not subordinate him or herself as an individual, he or she does contract away some minor rights and agrees that these will be used for the benefit of the company that employs them. If the employer lives up to his or her side of the agreement, the employee may not use his or her position against the interests of the firm.

CONFLICTS OF INTEREST

The interest of the firm is not always identical with the interest of the employee. This should surprise no one, for interests seldom coincide completely in any sphere of life. In general, the employees will think it to their interest to get the greatest possible reward for their work. The employer, on the other hand, sees his or her interest as identified in part with getting the greatest possible productivity out of the employees and machines. Because of this situation, the work contract is necessary to define the actual rights and interests of both parties. Each party gives up something in order to gain something. In this way, some conflicts can be avoided or at least minimized.

Conflicts of interest may be either actual or potential. As a result, certain actions that are not immediately harmful to the firm may be unethical because they contain the potentiality of a real conflict of interest or the possibility of destroying the good order of an entire industry. An actual conflict of interest exists when employees violate their contract of employment by using their position for selfish purposes that are at odds with the best interests of the firm. A purchasing agent who pays a higher price than necessary to a supplier from whom he has accepted a bribe is involved in an actual conflict of interest. On the other hand, a strong-minded individual who accepts large gifts may never actually harm the company, but she or he is still involved in a potential conflict of interest since most people in this sort of situation find it difficult to maintain their independence of judgment in acting for the true good of the company.

In many conflict of interest cases, not only the rights of the company but those of third parties are involved. It is necessary, then, to consider the impact of certain practices on parties outside the firm. For this reason, the questions of extortion and bribery are considered in the present chapter.

In studying conflicts of interest and related problems such as extortion, particular attention must be paid to the following:

1. The position of the individuals involved
2. The intentions of all parties
3. The impacts, potential and actual, on the parties, the company, and outside interests
4. Company policy, whether written or oral

BRIBERY, EXTORTION, AND GIFTS

The range of problems in this area of business ethics can be illustrated by a series of short cases, which contain nearly all of the relevant elements.

1. An art director for an advertising agency places his orders for supplies with a friend who "kicks back" a fixed percentage at the end of each month. The supplier's prices are fairly competitive, but the advertising agency does end up paying slightly more than necessary for its supplies.

The art director is accepting a *bribe* in taking a consideration for the performance of an act forbidden by his work contract. Even if his act did not cost the company money, he would be wrong since he is *cooperating* with another who intends to gain an unfair advantage, that is, preferential treatment not based on the merit of his product and prices. Since the company actually loses money because of this illegal contract, we are dealing with a form of *stealing*. Finally, such arrangements upset the orderly course of the industry and tempt others to engage in similar activities. The activity is also to be condemned because of its *broader effects.*

It should be noted that the method of payment does not change the intention or the effects of the bribery. Whether the consideration is in the form of cash, services, or privileges, we are dealing with bribery and a violation of the fiduciary relationship. Similarly, whether the consideration is given before or after the act, as a gift or as a loan that will never be repaid, the basic unethical quality remains so long as the intention is the same.

2. A purchasing agent will not even consider a salesman's offer unless he has received a substantial gift beforehand. Often he buys from the salesman who offers the best price, delivery, and quality, but occasionally he tosses some business to less competitive companies in order to keep their salesmen as contributors to his vacation fund.

This case involves not only bribery but *extortion.* Extortion exists when one demands payment of any sort for the execution (or non-execution) of acts which one is obliged to perform or to omit under the terms of one's work contract. Secondly, it is extortion to demand payment for the execution (or non-execution) of acts which an individual has no right to perform or to omit by virtue of his or her position. In its severest form, extortion may involve the use of physical force. Extortion in its mildest form may only involve implied threats unrelated to true business considerations.

Extortion includes all the evils of bribery plus the violation of the salesperson's right to fair and equal treatment based upon the merits of the product being sold. It violates the relationship between employer and employee and that between buyer and seller as well. If the salesperson offered the best product and service, the purchasing agent would be obliged to purchase from this seller without demanding personal profit. If the salesperson did not offer the best deal to the company, the agent had no right to give this seller the order after receiving the money that the agent had extorted.

Even though the extortioner may not harm his company in each and every transaction, the overall effect is one of serious violation of the fiduciary relationship. Indeed, if extortion becomes widespread, it will almost certainly force prices upward as bribes become fixed parts of the selling costs. Not merely the individual acts, but the ramifications must be considered if the evil effect is to be seen in all of its dimensions.

3. A department store manager accepts fairly substantial gifts such as cases of liquor from salespersons. The manager feels that these gifts do not prejudice his judgment. The company has a written policy against such gifts, but the manager justifies these actions on the ground that everyone does it.

Our third case does not necessarily involve either bribery or extortion. The manager does not intend to give favored treatment to those who fill the liquor cabinet, nor does the manager demand these gifts. It may even be that the salespersons do not expect to get favored treatment but only want to make sure that they get equal treatment. So long as the situation remains exactly as described, there is no actual conflict of interest as we have defined it earlier. None of this, however, should blind one to the real evils in the situation. Not only is there a *potential* conflict of interest, but there is a direct violation of company policy and of the work contract. The fact that others engage in the same practice increases rather than decreases the manager's obligation to avoid accepting substantial gifts. One individual's act sanctions the acts of others who, unknown to this person, may be involved in bribery, extortion, and real conflicts of interest. To put it another way, the store manager has an obligation to protect the best interests of the company by setting a good example as well as by having and demonstrating good intentions.

The salesperson may or may not intend the gifts as bribes. The manager has no reason to cooperate with what may be bribery. The store manager's cooperation in these actions serves to perpetuate a system that contributes nothing to good business and may be the breeding ground of seriously unethical practices.

Our case was fairly simple since the gifts were substantial, and there was an explicit company policy forbidding all gifts. When there is no clear policy, we are faced with questions like the following: At what point does a gift become so large or substantial that accepting it creates a potential conflict of interest? Under what circumstances, if any, does an employee have a proportionate reason for running the risks involved in accepting gifts? While there are no easy answers to these questions, the following considerations may be useful.

This basic question should be asked: "Will this gift, entertainment, or service cause any reasonable person to suspect my independence of judgment?" It should be clear that infrequent gifts of only a nominal cost, ten dollars or less, and small advertisement gifts will be acceptable unless forbidden by policy or law. On the other hand, practically any cash gift is liable to raise eyebrows and create a suspicion of bias.

Entertainment may be judged by similar norms. Industry custom may supply some guide lines, but one should be constantly aware of avoiding obligations that would hamper that independence of judgment necessary for fulfilling the responsibilities of the job. Some companies seek to minimize the problem by requiring employees to pick up the tab and turn it in for reimbursement. Others believe that reciprocity in entertainment will mitigate potential conflicts of interest. There is something to be said for both of these solutions, but reciprocity may merely authorize the mutual luncheon club in which members alternate in picking up the tab whether or not any *bona fide* business transaction has been involved.

In all cases of doubt, it is possible to get a ruling from the appropriate supervisor. If this includes full and honest disclosure of the problem, the employee has demonstrated his or her good faith by exposing his or her actions to surveillance. Many companies demand such disclosures as a standard procedure, and though it is not a panacea, it prevents the development of many dangerous situations. If nothing else, consultation and disclosure relieve the employee of nagging doubts and protect him or her against the deceptions of those who might want to involve the employee in a potential conflict of interest.

4. A salesperson who would never think of offering a bribe on his or her own finds himself or herself dealing with a customer who will not give serious consideration to an offer unless the customer's palm has been greased. The salesperson makes a contribution justifying it on the grounds that he or she must earn a living and is not really hurting the business.

Our fourth sample case involves cooperation with the unethical conduct of a customer who has resorted to extortion. While such cases may be solved on the principles given in Chapter Two, certain warnings are in order. The person cooperating may not *will* the harm as a means to his or her own ends. In judging whether or not he or she has a sufficient reason to *permit* the harm, the potential injury to the industry as well as to a particular company must be considered. Further, just making a sale is not a proportionate reason, for the salesperson's livelihood does not depend on getting this particular business. Finally, a *narrow* self-interest should always be suspected and countered lest easy rationalizations be used to excuse everything that suits one's fancy.

Cases of unethical cooperation often baffle younger business persons, since they may sense that something is wrong, but they lack the experience to identify the evil. They might remember that contact with evil tends to corrupt and caution is seldom out of order. At the same time, even the cautious person must realize that there are circumstances in which serious harm or the threat of it may justify his or her cooperating indirectly in a morally unsound transaction. The case we have just given cannot be solved without more information. However, the existence of a proportionate reason should be *proven* rather than assumed.

FINANCIAL AND OTHER INTERESTS

Sound ethics and many company policies seek to minimize potential conflicts of interest in the relations between supplier and producer as well as between agent and client. Typical company policies, for example, contain provisions like the following, promulgated by the International Harvester Company.[3]

> Thus, it is considered to be in conflict with the Company's interest:
> b . . . for an employee or member of his or her immediate family to benefit personally from any purchase of goods or services of whatever nature by the Company or its affiliates, or to derive personal gain from actions taken or associations made in his or her capacity as an employee of the Company;
> c . . . for an employee or member of his or her immediate family to have any interest, direct or indirect, in any organization which has

[3]*Business Ethics,* p. 12. A collection of documents compiled by the Research and Information Service of the American Management Association, 1963.

> business dealings with the Company or any affiliate, except when such interest comprises securities in widely held corporations and traded regularly in recognized security markets, and such interest is not in excess of 1% of the outstanding stock or other securities of such corporation, or except when such interest has been fully disclosed to the President of the Company for a determination as to the substantiality of such interest and the propriety of retaining it;
> d . . . for an employee to serve as an officer, director, employee or consultant of another company or organization which is a competitor of the Company or which is doing or seeking to do business with the Company or any affiliate, except that with the knowledge and consent of the President of the Company such employee may serve as a director of a corporation which is doing business with the Company, where no competitive situation is present;

The theory behind such policies should be obvious. Management and employees should avoid actual violations of their fiduciary relationships and situations which might weaken their independence of judgment and action. It should be noted that policies generally provide for exceptions that can be granted by the president and/or directors. There are reasons for this. No company wants to restrict its employees unnecessarily, and there are cases where the company itself can benefit by its employees' having interests in other companies.

The most subtle conflicts, both actual and potential, arise not because of a direct financial interest, but because of friendship or family loyalty. The problem is all the more difficult since both of these factors can often play a legitimate part in business. At the same time, there is danger that one hand may wash the other while the company's face gets dirty. It is not only a question of nepotism in hiring and leaking inside information but in giving out orders and making promotions on the basis of sentiment rather than of merit. Except in a family business, fairness to the company, employees, competing suppliers, and customers makes friendship and family suspect.

MOONLIGHTING

Paragraph *d* in the International Harvester policy points out several areas where moonlighting can be but is not necessarily hostile to company interests. Although the greatest problems arise when the second job is with a company that competes or deals with the primary employer, nearly all outside employment may involve some potential conflicts. If nothing else, a second job drains away energy, impairs efficiency, and divides interests. This does not mean that moonlighting is necessarily unethical. In many cases the employee has no choice. He or she must meet his obligations to his or her family, and therefore, barring an actual conflict of interest, the employee may have adequate reason for giving less than his or her all to the primary employer. Employers might give some thought to the fact that they get what they pay for and that they may be robbing themselves by underpaying their employees.

PREVENTING CONFLICTS OF INTEREST

Because there are so many gray areas, explicit company policy is useful if not absolutely necessary. Such policies will hardly deter the dishonest, but they give the decent individuals concrete norms that they can use in forming their values and in defending themselves against pressures. If nothing else, employees can give clear reasons for rejecting suspicious proposals.

Many companies try to lessen potential conflicts of interest by demanding from employees full disclosure of ownership in outside companies or of other relationships that might influence independence of judgment. Such disclosures can be of considerable help, but they probably need to be reinforced by periodic independent checks. In addition, the policy should be explicit so as to include all important sources of potential conflicts. Unfortunately, this may be impossible, for it is hard to legislate friendship and all family ties out of existence. At very least, one can try to explicate as clearly as possible the areas of danger that might require disclosure.

Often the temptation to become involved with conflicting interests is strongest for middle executives such as assistant purchasing agents or assistant department heads whose income may not be really commensurate with their responsibility and power. Since adequate pay can reduce this danger, companies should give serious consideration to this idea. Furthermore, a system of checks and balances in critical areas would seem to be in order. If even petty cash slips are a part of the company's standing control procedure, sensitive areas should be subject to some valid system of checks and balances.

As several studies have shown, the best protection is the example presented by the conduct of top management and the atmosphere it creates. When leaders are scrupulous, employees know what is considered right. When example is supported by explicit policy, the followers have a clear idea of how to translate the example of leaders into action. When policy is enforced and enforcement reinforced, the employees know that honesty is the best policy in this company.

EXECUTIVE PIRACY

We place the problem of executive piracy in the present chapter, since most of the cases that are unethical involve inducing a breach of contract or a violation of the fiduciary relationship. When the piracy has as its purpose the theft of secrets or the crippling of a competitor's business, there is no doubt about the unethical quality of the act. The real problems arise in those cases where the motive is not so clearly unethical.

When piracy involves tempting an individual to break a formal and explicit contract, it is generally unethical. However, if the recruiter and recruitee are only asking for a reconsideration and possibly a release from a contract, this can be ethical, since an employee does not lose the right to renegotiate and ask for release. Sometimes, we meet cases where the present employer has fulfilled all the technical parts of a work contract but violated its spirit. Ethically, we believe the employee in such circumstances is free to enter into a contract with a new employer. The legal aspects, however, need study by a lawyer. If we exclude the intention of hurting a competitor, we believe recruiters are ethically free to approach those ethically free to enter into a new contract.

Special problems arise when there is no formal agreement or contract but only a vague understanding that neither party regards as absolutely obligatory. To what extent is such an understanding binding in ethics if not in law? The employee, as we have noted in a previous chapter, has a reasonable expectation that he or she will not be fired except for just cause. So too, the employer has reasonable expectations that his or her personnel will not leave without good reason. This expectation can be particularly strong when the employer has taken on the burden of training and has kept on an employee through rough times. While such factors may not create a legal obligation in the absence of a formal contract, they certainly enter into the calculation of proportionality.

The factors mentioned above are often outweighed by both individual and social reasons. It is important that human resources be allocated properly and not frozen in a position where their true economic and creative potential cannot be fully realized. Furthermore, unless the employee has some freedom to better himself, the employment contract might be a modern form of peonage. Legally, people can enter into contracts that stipulate that they are not to compete for a period of time or in a given area. Thus, the employment contract may contain a provision that an employee may not work for a rival during a period of two years after the termination of his or her job. If the contract is truly free and legal, there is an obligation to observe it. We should, however, recognize the possibility that this may not be in the true public interest.

Non-recruiting pacts, like blacklists, are socially harmful, illegal, and potentially unjust to employees. Indeed, unless companies are challenged to make the best use of their human resources, they too may suffer from tired managerial blood. Furthermore, unless there are periodic occasions where the market sets the price of management talent, a company can be underpaying. Actually, many problems in this area may be mitigated if a company has a policy of using formal contracts that are temporarily binding; they allow the company to recover its recruiting and training costs, and give it the option of matching *bona fide* offers from other companies. While such contractual provisions are not a final solution, they do help to regularize the expectations of both employee and employer.

The words bona fide in the previous paragraph are important, since some offers are obtained by employees only as a means of forcing employers into paying higher salaries. The line between the ethical and the unethical is very fine in this area. The ethical problem can be resolved, to a large extent, once the fairness of the employee's present salary and the sincerity of the employee's new job offer have been determined. Actually, many such problems can be solved if recruiters inform employers of their intention of approaching an employee. When transactions are aboveboard, the possibility of a free and honest agreement resulting is increased. Unfortunately, disclosure of other job opportunities can expose employees to such retaliation as firing or the refusal of letters of recommendation. There are cases where vindictive employers have raised an employee's salary to meet the competition and then fired the individual as soon as the job in the other company had been filled.

Because there are some selfish and spiteful individuals in business, it must be remembered that the principle of proportionality excuses innocent parties from exposing themselves to many risks. Young men and women who have come from the neat, clean world of the college may find corruption disconcerting, but business embraces individuals of every stamp. While candor and openness are certainly admirable qualities, the prudent person must make sure not to be naive. In any event, it is always well to know the persons with whom one is dealing and then make a careful judgment as to what is to be done.

Despite our inability to settle all problems, we can see that several forms of piracy are unethical: those which are aimed at stealing secrets and crippling business, as well as those which lead to unlawful breach of contract or of the fiduciary relationship.

Employers who fear pirating will do well to examine both their corporate policies and their own consciences. It is not easy to lure a contented worker who is adequately paid and finds both his or her present work and future prospects humanly satisfying. The company that underpays an employee or does not give him or her a sense of growth is asking for trouble and deserves it when it comes.

BY WAY OF SUMMARY

While the concrete situation demands the consideration of a fairly large number of pertinent circumstances, the principal question remains the same: "What is due to those with whom I deal?" A precise understanding of the demands of the work contract is essential if this question is to be satisfactorily answered. The contract does not give all the answers; additional questions are necessary. Will my actions impede my independence of judgment in doing my job? Will my contemplated actions lead others to engage in unethical activities? Even if my intention is ethical, is there any proportionate reason for risking or permitting harm to outsiders such as the stockholders and the competitors of the firms with which I must deal?

7

SECRECY AND ESPIONAGE

INTRODUCTION

As information becomes more and more vital in business, secrecy becomes a major ethical concern. The use of insider information, the growth of commercial espionage, and the promotion of screening methods have called attention to the problem of information control. Because nearly everyone in a company has some access to valuable information, the ethics of secrecy touches both the president of the firm and the person who empties the wastebaskets.

A secret is knowledge which one has a right and/or an obligation to keep hidden. The most important secrets involve both a right and an obligation. These *obligatory secrets* always involve situations in which revelation of the knowledge would cause serious harm or the violation of a contract. For the purpose of analysis, we may divide these obligatory secrets into three general categories. In order of ascending significance they are

1. The natural secret
2. The promised secret
3. The professional secret

A comment on each will provide us with an analytic tool for handling some of the more common cases in business.

The *natural secret* involves knowledge of something that, by its nature, will cause harm if revealed. For example, an employer who knows that a worker has a criminal record realizes that the publication of this fact will make the employee's life difficult. Unless there is a *proportionate reason* for revealing the information, such knowledge is to be kept hidden. This duty of secrecy exists no matter how the information was gathered, since the harm results from the revelation even when the knowledge was obtained ethically.

Generally speaking, the *promised secret* involves a natural secret. The obligation to keep it, however, arises not only from the nature of the matter but from the promise or contract by which one binds oneself. Many business secrets are of this sort, since they arise from conditions explicit or implicit in the work contract. Although such secrets are obligatory aside from the nature of the matter, they too may be revealed when silence will cause more harm than good. An employee with knowledge of the company secrets may be allowed to reveal these to save an innocent party from harm or to protect him or herself from an unjust accusation.

The *professional secret* involves not only an implied promise and a natural secret, but the reputation of a group whose services are necessary for society. Clergymen, doctors, lawyers, and accountants can serve society only if people feel free to give them highly confidential information. If a public accountant reveals the secrets of a client, he or she injures the whole system of business by reducing confidence in the profession. For this reason, only the most serious reasons can justify the revelation of a professional secret. There may even be cases where a professional man must risk personal ruin rather than violate a trust.

As noted above, any one of the secrets can be revealed when silence will cause more harm than good. This is in line with the general principles developed at the beginning of this book. Three warnings, however, are in order. First, even when a revelation is justified, it must be made in such a way as to *minimize harm*. A company physician who knows that someone has a communicable disease has to report to the proper authorities, but the doctor is not free to tell others unless this is necessary to protect the innocent.

Second, we may reveal a secret to protect ourselves from a proportionate harm but not to gain some advantage to which we have no right. Thus, one may reveal the fact that another person has a drinking problem if one is being blamed for not doing work that is really this individual's responsibility. On the other hand, one would be wrong in revealing the same fact if one's only motive were the removal of a potential rival for a promotion. The phrasing, "to protect ourselves from a proportionate harm," is important, since the principle does not justify revelations for any and all causes.

Third, a secret can be revealed by action as well as by word or gesture. The executive who uses insider information for personal gain has revealed a secret even though he has not even told his wife why he acted as he did.

The natural and promised secret may be ethically revealed if the person who would be harmed and/or the person who exacted the promise freely would give permission upon reasonable cause. In some cases, even the professional secret may be revealed with proper permission. Great care and discretion, however, are necessary in the revelation of the professional secret. Unless the fact of permission is known to others, confidence in the profession may still be shaken. For this reason some professionals insist that the permission be given in writing.

NON-OBLIGATORY SECRETS

There are secrets that we have a *right but not an obligation to keep.* There is *no* obligation to hide the fact that one's father came from a very poor family, but one has a right to keep this to oneself. If a person invents a new method for making steel cheaply, this person, as a private individual, is not obliged to keep this secret, but may do so. The owner of a business may reveal his or her cost figures to the public if he or she wishes, but the owner is not obliged to do so under ordinary circumstances. This is merely to say that one has much *information that one may either reveal or keep secret.*

This right of secrecy is not unlimited. It may meet the claims of others and create an obligation to reveal information. Thus, a seller is obliged to reveal substantial defects to a buyer. A citizen may be obliged to reveal his or her income to the government, although not to a neighbor. One may be obliged to reveal information the suppression of which would cause grave harm to society or to a large group of people. One may thus have *information that one would like to keep secret but have an obligation to reveal,* at least to some people in some situations.

Finally, there is information that one has no obligation to reveal but which *others may rightfully seek to obtain* by ethical means. This is the case where one possesses information *but does not have a strict property right* to it. The list of one's customers is something one may keep to oneself, but it is also something a competitor may seek to find out providing he or she does not steal private papers, break into property, and unethically violate privacy.

Unfortunately, the line between information that one *possesses* and information that one *owns* is often difficult to draw. As a result, there will be areas in which it will be difficult to decide who is in the right.

INSIDER INFORMATION

By the work contract, an employee promises to keep secret information that would harm the firm if revealed. When the employee is an officer or manager, that employee also promises implicitly to protect the rights of stockholders for whom he or she is an agent or trustee. This is clearly concerned with the areas of insider information.

The use of insider information could have been treated in the chapter on the fiduciary relationship, since this relationship underlies the obligation to keep insider information inside. Much information belongs to an employee or an officer of a corporation only by virtue of his or her job and is to be used for the good of the corporation and not for personal profit. For example, a person knows that the company is about to purchase a certain piece of property. If that person buys the property through a dummy and then raises the price, the individual has used the resources of the corporation against the corporation. Such a person has also violated his or her obligation to secrecy since this person revealed—to him or herself in the role of agent for personal interest—information entrusted to them in the role of employee. This may seem a strange way to put it, but it underlines the fact that we may often have to compartmentalize our lives if we are to be ethical.

Sometimes the use of insider information does not directly harm the company but injures present and future stockholders. Thus, company officers and directors who buy their company's stock because they know of an announcement that will dramatically raise the value of the stock cheat the people from whom they buy the stock. The fiduciary relationship of these individuals to the company obliges them to keep secret everything that they know because of their official position. If the same officers spread rumors to depress the value of the stock so that they may buy it at a lower price, they harm not only the seller but the company and all its stockholders even if the rumor is true.

Not only the use of insider information but the revelation of "trade secrets" can be both illegal and unethical. The "trade secrets" to be guarded include just about everything that will affect the competitive position of the firm: formulae, inventions; manufacturing and marketing processes, organizational and motivational schemes, lists of customers, and codes for determining discounts and rebates. Even when the revelation of such secrets does not violate explicit contractual provisions, such revelations are so disruptive of the trust needed for good employee/firm relations that it is almost always unethical.[1]

CASES

In the actual world of business, even the most loyal and honest executives find themselves faced with difficult problems. A few examples will serve to illustrate the dilemmas of the honest business person.

1. Company A has a regular policy of buying up its own stock to be listed in its accounts as treasury stock, to be included in its pension portfolio, or to be sold to executives who have a stock option. The directors know that the value of the stock will rise dramatically when certain discoveries and innovations are announced to the public. May they authorize the company to buy up an extra large block of its own stock immediately before the announcement in order to reduce the costs to the company?

2. An executive is in charge of investing ten million dollars a year for the company's pension fund. A stockbroker who specializes in finding unlisted stock

[1]For an interesting discussion of trade secrets and their impact on the economy as a whole see Russell B. Stevenson, Jr., *Corporations and Information: Secrecy, Access and Disclosure* (Baltimore: The Johns Hopkins University Press, 1980).

with great potential informs him that he or she has knowledge which indicates a certain company is a "sleeper." May the corporate executive act on this information or is he or she cooperating in an unethical use of insider information?

3. A stockholder, ignorant of the true value of the company, offers to sell his or her stock to the company treasury at a price well below its true value. The company accepts his offer. Is this an ordinary business transaction or has there been real exploitation since full disclosure of the facts might have been made?

4. A company, having discovered valuable deposits in northern Canada, offers the present owner of the land the current market value saying nothing about the real value of the property. Is this shrewd but ethical business or exploitation?

In the first case, the company's policy of buying a certain number of shares regularly for the purposes stated need not be changed because of insider information, since the information *has not motivated* the regular purchase. However, when it decides to *increase* its purchase because of the insider information, it is taking advantage of the ignorance of its own stockholders for whom it is, after all, the agent. This is to say that the officers violate their fiduciary relationship to their own stockholders. The public use of the information is not ethical until the information is communicated to all those who have a right to it.

It should be noted that the misuse of information of this sort can injure not only present stockholders but potential buyers and the confidence necessary for the orderly conduct of the stock market itself. As we shall see in a later chapter, customers have rights to certain information and concealment can be unethical in many circumstances. In any event, the use of insider information involves more than injury to the firm and its owners.

In the second example, the ethical quality of the corporation's actions will depend on the answers to the following questions: 1. Did the broker obtain real insider information? 2. How did he or she obtain it?

It may be that the information is actually available to the public although it has not been widely diffused. In such a case, we cannot see any ethical problem, since both the broker and the pension fund officer are using a publicly available means. Often too, the knowledge or information may be the result of a shrewd deduction. For example, the broker may know that a very talented officer is about to enter the company, or he or she may have deduced, from public records of land purchases, that the company has made a valuable discovery. Such information is really public with the result that there is no ethical problem.

The means by which the information is obtained are often ethically significant. If any of the unethical means mentioned in previous chapters have been used, the entire operation is certainly suspect. Situations are not always quite this simple, however. The broker may have overheard something at a cocktail party, or the company may have fed him the information for its own purposes. In these cases, we must ask if the broker is obliged to keep quiet, since he or she is certainly not bound by any fiduciary relationship with the company in question.

In view of the various possibilities, we would venture the following tentative opinion. The company executive who is going to act on the broker's tip should not fear cooperation in the unethical use of insider information *unless he has some good reason* to suspect that the information was obtained or disclosed unethically. Even when he or she has founded suspicions that someone else has acted unethically without his or her encouragement or permission, we believe this individual may sometimes have a proportionate reason for using the information. There are cases where this person's failure to act may cost the company a great deal without protecting others from the harm.

In our third case, where the stockholder makes an offer to the company while ignorant of the true value of the stock, the directors may accept the offer in good faith if they are not free to reveal the true value of the company to all stockholders. On the other hand, if the information should be in the hands of all stockholders, they are exploiting the ignorance of this particular individual.

The fourth case, which involves the purchase of property from an owner ignorant of its true value, is different from the previous cases in two important respects. First, the company does not have a fiduciary relationship with the potential seller, as it did with its stockholders. Secondly, whereas the stockholders were in no position to get the information legitimately unless they got it from the officers, the potential seller of the land can, if he or she wishes to spend the money, get the same information. To put it another way, the stockholder has a right to the information because he or she has helped to pay for it, whereas the seller of the land has no right to information paid for by others. One might note in passing that if the company informed the landowner of the true value of the land, it would be violating its fiduciary relationship to its own stockholders.

A seller, as we shall see in a later chapter, may have an obligation to reveal certain defects to a buyer. A buyer, however, is under no obligation to reveal hidden advantages to the seller unless, of course, the buyer is also acting as an appraiser or even as an agent for the seller, as in the case of a corporation buying from its own stockholders.

In this context, it is well to note that the government is in a slightly different position when it acts as a buyer. Public officials must use their insider information for the common good of the whole of society. If the information is revealed, it must be revealed to everyone at the same time, since no group has a right to preferment in these cases. Leaking information on proposed road construction can be very unethical, since it can not only raise the prices which government must pay, but deprive owners of the value which will accrue to their property when a public announcement is made.

These few cases on insider information indicate the need for great care in analyzing the obligation of secrecy as it exists in varying relationships. In particular, attention should be given to the impact of revelations, to the means used in getting the information, and to the rights, or lack of rights, of the various parties involved.

While we have used illustrative cases involving high-ranking company officials, even such lower echelon employees as a switchboard operator may have access to valuable inside information. Indeed, a nosy and, therefore, unethical switchboard operator may be the best informed person in the firm. Secretaries too should remember that their work contract calls for secrecy; they should be on their guard against those who would seek information from them. Silence is generally golden.

OBLIGATIONS OF FORMER EMPLOYEES

The previous paragraphs apply to those who are *actually* employed by a company. Employees leave, however, and they take valuable information with them. What part of this information may they use or sell to others? What part of this information can a competitor ethically try to elicit from the former employee of a rival?

A person may not use or sell information that is the *property* of a former employer without permission. To do so would be stealing. A person may not use or sell information that he or she has freely agreed not to use or sell after termination of the employment. To do so could be a violation of a contract. Other knowledge, which is not the former employer's property and is not the object of a contractual agreement, may be used or sold by an employee when the employee leaves. In other words, with the two exceptions given above, trade secrets are not ethically binding after the termination of employment.

These statements are clear enough, but they can be difficult to apply either because contracts are vague or because it is hard to decide when a person has a *property right* in information or knowledge.

Companies can solve some problems if there are clear and precise contractual provisions covering the use of information gained during the course of employment. If nothing else, such contracts can help the honest employee to form his or her own conscience. The question of a property right in either an idea or information is not so easily resolved although the laws of copyright and patents may provide some guide lines. In any event, legal advice is often necessary in the extensive grey area surrounding trade secrets. While further statutory law might help to clarify this area, such laws ought to consider the broad impact of secrecy on the public interest as well as on the business firms.

SECRECY AND THE PUBLIC INTEREST

In general, society profits from the wide diffusion of useful knowledge. The concealment of such information and its exclusive possession tend to give some groups power over others. Modern science has made many of its advances because people felt that the results of research belonged to all members of the scientific community and ultimately to all humanity. There is good justification for such a view, since knowledge itself is the result of a social process as well as of individual efforts and brilliance. This is particularly true today when so much of our basic research is sponsored by the government or by great universities, which are the agents of the general society. Even the brilliant theorist who works without laboratory and assistants builds on the research and insights of those who have gone before. In view of this, it is difficult to see how any person or group of people can claim exclusive control of any knowledge that might be socially useful.

Secrecy and the control of information may be very profitable, but the social effects of this are of questionable value. The knowledge which is buried because it might obsolete a company's present line of products robs society of real benefits. The cost figures that are kept secret may protect a company against competitors, but the secrecy may also rob society of means by which to judge the true efficiency of a firm and the fairness of its prices. The concealment of plans to relocate may save the company a long period of complaints from the community, but it may leave the community unprepared for a serious crisis. Exclusive knowledge of a new drug may help a company to recover its research costs, yet the company may be tempted to charge very high prices for an item that people really need.

All of these considerations raise questions concerning the revelation of facts traditionally held to be business secrets. Questions as to whether or not a man should have a property right in an idea are also significant here. Society may see fit to protect man in the enjoyment of the fruits of his thinking, research, and ingenuity. However, he should not be protected at the expense of society. The social interest in a wide diffusion of knowledge would seem to justify the use and sale of information belonging to a former employer in most cases where there is any doubt about the existence of a strict property right in information.

COMMERCIAL ESPIONAGE

The growth of commercial espionage and of services devoted to ferreting out business secrets bears witness to the increasing utility of information in business. It also creates ethical problems both in regard to the information that can be legitimately gathered and the methods by which it is collected.

It is stealing to buy or use information to which someone else has a strict property right unless the owner gives permission. It will also be unethical to hire away an employee in order to obtain information that is either the property of another or the object of a contract forbidding revelation. Much business information, of course, is covered by neither a property right nor a contract.

When this is the case, the ethical problems will concern the means used rather than the information itself.

The use of bribery, theft, trespass, and fraud is unethical. Also, methods that violate privacy by the use of wire taps and similar devices are generally to be condemned. However, if we prescind from the law, which can make certain acts illegal and unethical, there may be cases where extreme measures could be justified in order to protect clear rights. These cases would be rare, since they would occur only when a business person had good reason to suspect that a competitor was planning to use illegal or unethical means against them. To put it another way, there would have to be a situation of almost unlimited war rather than normal competition. This is to say that unjust and unethical attacks can so change the nature of competition that an honest business person may have a proportionate reason for using extreme measures that would be unethical in ordinary, fair competition. It should be noted, however, that the ethics of self-defense or warfare demand that the attack be unjust and that all normal means of defense, such as the courts, should have been tried before extreme measures are taken. This follows from the principles of Chapter One—governing proportionality and alternate means. The law, of course, should always be consulted. Indeed, it is desirable that there be stricter laws covering the large number of gray areas that may develop.

While a large number of methods in actual use are to be condemned, there are legitimate means of gathering information about competitors. A competitor's customers are *ordinarily* not bound by any form of secrecy and are sources of valuable information about sales. This same is true of suppliers who know some vital cost figures and specifications. However, both of these may be bound by agreements, so a fiduciary relationship is not ruled out entirely.

Ordinarily surveillance, which does not involve fraud or trespass, also seems to be acceptable. If the actions of a competitor are public enough to be observed by ordinary watchfulness, then the information gained would appear to be public. If the competitor wants to keep things secret, he or she must take reasonable precautions to maintain his privacy.

The terms "ordinary" and "reasonable" should cause no problem in understanding, but their application does raise difficulties. The existence of sophisticated devices, which can monitor conversations through open windows or through walls with no physical trespass, makes it extremely difficult, if not impossible, to protect privacy. Furthermore, because the use of such devices is becoming prevalent, there is a temptation to call them ordinary. Technological advance has created new gray areas. While the present writers are almost instinctively against the use of devices that violate privacy with or without trespass, there are many cases that can only be settled by careful legislation. In the absence of such law, companies will have to take increasing care in the protection of their secrets.

OBLIGATIONS OF THE EMPLOYER

The employer, too, has an obligation to keep secret a great deal of information about the employee. In some cases the obligation arises because the information is particularly harmful, or because it was obtained under an implicit contract which limits its use. Health reports, psychological and psychiatric tests, secret investigations of the employee's credit and activities—all fall under this obligation. Even though the information was obtained ethically, it must still be used ethically. It should be kept in closed files available only to those in the company who really need the information for making decisions. Also, such information may not be made public without the permission of the employee. This means that the information may not be passed on to future employers or to government agencies without permission. Unethical procedures may leave the employer open to suit for a violation of privacy. The law in this area is not entirely clear, but it will probably tend to give increased protection to the individual's right to privacy and to his or her reputation.

JOB RECOMMENDATIONS

The principles given above may seem to pose a problem for those who must write letters of recommendation. However the problem in minimized if a distinction is made between public and private information. Public information is gained by ordinary observation of work performance, intelligence, honesty, and motivation. It is available to anyone who cares to look. Private information, on the other hand, is gained only through a confidential relationship. This information includes test results, school marks, and investigations into private matters. While an employee, in view of his or her position, may willingly permit the company to acquire this information, he or she does not make it a part of the public record. If others want this information, they too must get the individual's permission.

Even public information, which has not been widely disseminated, may pose an ethical problem when some of it is potentially harmful to the employee. This may not be distributed except to individuals who have a legitimate interest in it. By legitimate interest we mean that the individual needs the information to make a proper decision about hiring or promoting a person. The fact that someone has a legitimate interest in information that is potentially harmful *does not necessarily mean that there is an obligation to provide it*. Indeed, there are cases where it should not be provided. In the first place, if the potential harm outweighs any possible good resulting from the transmission, it would seem obligatory to remain silent. In the second place, there are cases where a person can be sued for defamation because of an unfavorable letter. Prudence would dictate great caution where such a danger exists even though ethics might say there is a sufficient reason for revelation.

Although there is ordinarily no obligation to give even public information about an employee except by his request, there is an obligation to write truthful letters once a person has volunteered or agreed to do so. A letter of recommendation that omits pertinent but unfavorable items can do considerable harm. It may not only encourage another to hire an unsuitable employee but possibly deprive a more qualified applicant of a job. Furthermore, it can undermine confidence in the writer even though what he did say was true. Once again a thoughtful consideration of all factors is in order.

In practice, there are three simple rules that go far towards assuring fairness. First, the recommender should use only the results of his or her own observations. Rumor and hearsay should not be used. Second, only information relevant to the new job should be provided. Third, only habitual faults should be included. The rare exception might occur if the employee has been convicted of a crime which would affect his or her business performance. In general, however, isolated instances of behavior are not of great significance and should not be included.

BY WAY OF SUMMARY

The present chapter is filled with references to gray areas because there are so many new problems on which there is no body of careful thought. Despite this, the principles given should cover most of the cases met in business. In every case, the decision maker should consider the basic set of questions given in Chapter One and then use the material given in this chapter for determining proportionality. It will also be useful to check the nature and extent of the rights of all parties involved, since these rights are often either overlooked or exaggerated.

8

HONESTY AND EXPENSE ACCOUNTS

INTRODUCTION

There is much concern about dishonesty in the office and in the plant. Some estimate that petty thievery costs American business billions every year. While it is impossible to document this, there are cases where the theft of small articles has amounted to hundreds of thousands of dollars in a single firm. Purchasing agents admit that, in August, they put in large orders for pencils, notebooks, and the like, since there is a big drain on supplies when school opens. Sometimes, the losses result from organized theft; at other times the blame falls on the individual who uses the company's postage meter to mail out Christmas cards. The employee who punches another's time card and the executive who uses company maintenance staff to paint his house are equally dishonest. One way or another, theft is a serious moral and business problem.

Ethicians define theft as "taking what belongs to another when he or she is reasonably unwilling." Each of the key words in this definition must be understood if stealing as an ethical category is to be isolated. In the first place, the word "other" refers to both real and moral persons. While the company may seem to be an impersonal being without a face, it is a moral being with a right to its own property. Ultimately, moreover, theft from the company is theft from real persons such as owners, stockholders, fellow employees, and the owners of insurance companies.

Obviously there is no theft if, for example, the real owner *freely* permits me to take something. If it is his to give, his willingness transfers the title to me. The owner of a business can give regular permission for taking home small supplies and even for the private use of facilities. Sometimes the permission is explicit; sometimes it is expressed in knowing toleration of custom. The mode of expression is not important providing that the owner has signified willingness to give the item to the employee.

However, employees often see willingness where there is none. The owner or the manager may be very much opposed to "borrowing" but refrains from saying anything lest he cause discontent. In such cases, the employer's silence is not consent. Indeed, it may be seething fury in the face of theft compounded by petty blackmail. If the employee has any doubt, let him or her ask. If the employee hesitates to ask, this is a fairly clear sign that he or she knows that the other is unwilling.

Since being unwilling is not the same as being reasonably unwilling, the employee might ask him or herself what his or her opinion would be if roles were reversed. Neither of these methods is infallible, but they will expose much of the rationalization that is used to justify theft. At the same time, the owner is not *reasonably* unwilling if the employee is taking what is his or her right by contract. The typical case occurs when the employer does not pay the agreed wages, and the employee, having no way of winning a case in court, "simply takes" his or her wages. Similar situations can occur with regard to fringe benefits and working conditions.

It should be noted that non-owner managers do not have an unlimited right to give away company property in ordinary circumstances. They, after all, are only agents. As a result, the willingness of a manager who does not have the right to alienate goods is most often not permission but cooperation in theft. Similarly, custom should be scrutinized lest accumulated bad habits be taken as the authorization of theft. Too many people are willing to justify themselves on the grounds that it is part of the game, without realizing that the game may be crooked.

The true owner must be *reasonably unwilling* that the object be taken. Obviously it is not theft to take a gun from a madman or a child no matter how unwilling he may be. Thus, there may be objects of little or no value that the owner would not reasonably object to being taken. Even here, however, it is easy to form a false conscience. A single pencil may be worth very little, but when a large number is taken, the accumulated loss may be considerable, with the result that the owner is quite reasonably unhappy about the situation.

It is often difficult to draw the line. However, because both our moral sense and the rights of others can be eroded subtly over the course of time, it is the owner who should be given the benefit of the doubt and not the would-be thief. After all, the owner does have a good title to his own goods, and a congenial suspicion that he might not object strenuously does not constitute good title.

For these reasons, and in the absence of permission, the use of the company meter for personal mail and the continued borrowing of pens and erasers are forms of theft. The evil is found not merely in the violation of another's rights to his own goods, but in the fact that even small thefts impair the whole fabric of trust, which is one of the essential structures of both business and society in general.

OBLIGATIONS OF OWNERS AND MANAGERS

Owners and managers have serious obligations in this area. In the first place, they should set a good example lest employees, operating on the principle of what is sauce for the goose is sauce for the gander, imitate their superiors in petty theft. The double standard in this area can only encourage dishonesty. In addition, employers have an obligation to protect their goods, and they should also protect their workers from unnecessary temptation. While most people may be honest at the onset, temptation can wear resolve thin and swell the ranks of amateur thieves. It may cost money to put in a proper protection system. The money, however, is not merely an ordinary operating expense, but an investment in maintaining the integrity of the work force.

In addition, employers should be certain that their policies are forcefully articulated, since silence is often taken as consent. When theft is detected, serious consideration should be given not merely to firing but to prosecuting in the courts. The lack of stern measures has often encouraged continued dishonesty. Worse yet, there are cases on record where employers have given recommendations to dishonest employees. Perhaps sentimentality will condone such practices. Ethics, however, must condemn them, since theft disrupts the workings of business and exposes innocent people to unnecessary losses.

EXPENSE ACCOUNTS

The much discussed question of expense accounts deals with the ethics of stealing. The fact of theft is often concealed by the absence of face to face contact and by the bookkeeping system, but stealing is stealing. Problems involving expense accounts arise from three relationships: the relationship of the recipient to the company, the relationship of the grantor to the recipient and the company, and the relationship of the recipient and the company to the tax laws.

Expense accounts can be divided into the following three general policies:

1. A flat allowance whether *annual* or *per diem* is given to the employee.
2. The employee is directly reimbursed for expenses already incurred.
3. The employee charges his or her expenses, and the company reimburses the seller. This form is often combined with the second.

THE FLAT ALLOWANCE

For the flat expense allowance, whether *annual* or *per diem,* the employee need not make an accounting. The allowance, however, is to be used for the good of the company. The employee who hurts the company's reputation by skimping is not fulfilling his or her implied contract. In some cases, the company may even intend the allowance as a hidden form of compensation so that the employee may pocket the difference between actual expenses and the flat sum. It should be noted that this difference or residue must be reported as income, since there is still a duty to pay one's taxes.

Although most cases involve an employee's abuse of an expense account, the company can also offend. Unrealistically low expense allowances can force the employee to pay for necessary and ordinary expenses out of his or her own pocket. If pressure is used to enforce such arrangements, there is a polite form of extortion. Careful analysis must be used in these cases for there are many legitimate arrangements whereby a company only pays part of the expenses. If this is understood by both parties from the very start and no coercion is used, there would appear to be no injustice.

REIMBURSEMENT DIRECTLY TO THE EMPLOYEE

When an employee must put in a claim for expenses actually incurred, there may be real moral problems. First, there is the problem of truthful reporting and second of just title to the money. The resolution of cases in both these areas depends in large part on company policy. Such policy sets forth the terms of the contract and informs the employee how he shall report and what he may claim. In general, an employee has right and title to reimbursement for his or her expenses if all three of the following conditions have been met. First, the money was actually spent. Second, it was spent on behalf of the company. Third, it was spent with at least the implicit permission if not at the direct request of the company.

Company policies generally specify that employees should live as comfortably on the road as at home and should not suffer any monetary loss because of their work. When there is no company policy, an employee can safely follow the norm just given, since it reflects sound business and ethical thinking. Obviously this is a flexible norm whose precise content varies with the income and position of the employee. It is, nevertheless, a useful rule-of-thumb for both employers and employees. Of course, there are times when the company may want to make an impression and authorize better transportation and accommodations. This is its privilege within the limits set by the Internal Revenue Service.

Some employees are tempted to claim more than they have actually spent on the grounds that they had a right to spend more. It is argued that the company will make no objection, so long as the total bill is not too far out of line. Hence it is not stealing if the employee pockets the fruits of his or her own economy. This position may be justified if the practice has been explicitly approved by the proper authorities. However, two points should be kept in mind. The economy, which benefits the employee, does not benefit the company and may harm it. Second, unless the company freely makes a gift to the employee, he or she has no title to the money. In this type of expense account, the title arises only from the fact that money has been legitimately spent on behalf of the company.

Although the company can reimburse all legitimate expenses, it cannot claim a deduction against its taxes unless the expenditure is reasonable and necessary for the ordinary course of business. In addition, the expenditure must be substantiated in a satisfactory manner and have some definite and approximate relationship to the particular business enterprise. This is merely to say that the legal aspect must be considered in ethical problems involving expense accounts.

Because the law must be considered, certain practices which are ethical in the abstract may not be permissible in the concrete. So long as the employee has spent the total sum claimed on behalf of the firm, the sub-headings he or she uses in preparing his account may not be too important from an ethical point of view. However, if he reports expenses not deductible by law under headings that make them deductible, he or she may cause the accounting department to make illegal claims.

The third type of expense account, in which the employee charges his or her expenses and the company reimburses the seller or credit service, poses no ethical difficulties in addition to those treated, except for the problem of cooperation in theft. This question will be treated later.

DOUBLE EXPENSE ACCOUNTS

A case involving the double expense account will illustrate some of the more difficult expense account problems. A young man is invited to New York for interviews by two different companies, both of which offer to pay his expenses. The recruitee bills both companies for the full expense of the trip, thus making a very nice profit. He justifies himself on the grounds that both companies were willing to pay and that, if he had to make two trips, he could legitimately have made two claims. Although there is some dispute in this case, we see this as stealing, since the title to reimbursement arises not from the trip, but from the incurrence of the expenses. While an individual is entitled to have his expenses covered, he is not ordinarily supposed to make a profit.

If one of the companies makes an outright offer of payment practically in the form of a gift, the recruitee may bill the other company because he has two separate titles: the title of gift and the title of expenses legitimately incurred. We feel that the intention to make a gift should be proved rather than assumed as a ready-made excuse for lining one's pockets. Of course, the problem would not arise at all if companies asked for substantiation of all major expenses. Unfortunately, carelessness can introduce the prospective employee to temptation even before he is hired.

Similar cases can arise in advertising, public relations, and accounting firms whose representatives may be servicing more than one client on a given trip. When the problem is going to arise frequently, there is need for a policy that either prorates the expenses or assigns them on some basis—such as the primary purpose of the trip and whether or not a particular client requested the trip in the first place.

THE SPOUSE ON THE EXPENSE ACCOUNT

Company policies on the spouse traveling with an employee vary widely. The principle underlying the policy seems, however, to be the same: The company will pay for the spouse who is performing some service for the company. To put it another way, the company will authorize the expenses for the spouse when they are also tax-deductible. Even when the expense is not tax-deductible, as directly and immediately related to the good of the firm, the company can reasonably authorize such expenses on its own when long and frequent absences from home may damage the morale of the employee. It is difficult, however, to see where such expenses are tax-deductible. It should be noted that, as a rule, companies grant the privilege frequently to top executives, with middle management being given the privilege only occasionally. In many cases, the company will pay for the spouse only when it has requested his or her presence.

Sometimes employees take their spouses and bill the company although much of the expense was not incurred by the employee. This is done by taking a double room in a slightly less expensive hotel, by flying tourist instead of first class, and by eating in slightly less expensive places than when the employee travels alone. This system does not cost the company one cent extra, since the employee pays whatever expenses are incurred over the normal or allowed expenses. Despite this, the present writers feel that in the absence of approval by the company, the employee has no title to more than was actually spent on the company's behalf. Some may consider this unduly rigorous; but in an area where it is so easy to deceive oneself, it is best to stick by principle. If the employee really feels a need to have the spouse along despite company policy, the employee is always free to pay out of his or her own pocket.

COMPANY POLICY

The cases we have discussed indicate that good company policy can do much to help employees form sound ethical judgments and to maintain control of expenses. A good policy must conform to the tax laws, but it also must respect both the needs of the employees and the best interests of the company.

Company policy should forbid paying an employee's salary through the expense account. First, if this is not forbidden, the employee may be tempted to cheat the government by not reporting his or her true income. Second, employees should be paid what they are worth directly rather than through hidden forms of compensation that may be illegal and may deceive stockholders as to true salary costs.

Company policy should forbid practices that force the employee to pay costs that should be borne by the firm. It should, in short, provide for equitable reimbursement. This involves constant updating of allowances in an economy characterized by a rising cost of living.

While the owner of a company need maintain only those controls demanded by the Internal Revenue Service, non-owner managers may have more serious obligations. Our tax laws may create the impression that the government pays for part of the expense account, but the cost to the company is real. Since the non-owner manager is handling other people's money, he or she should be sure that the company policy does not authorize waste. In any company, expenses should be controlled since expense accounts can be used to obtain money for bribery and other unethical practices. Sound business practice would dictate documentation and periodic audit of all expenses.

COOPERATION IN THEFT

In many cases, abuse of expense accounts and other forms of theft are possible only because of the cooperation of individuals either inside or outside the company. Thus, restaurants which supply salespeople with fictitious, inflated bills to present for reimbursement are cooperating in theft even though the restaurant gets no more than its normal return on a given sale. This is true whether the transaction is in cash or through the medium of a credit card or an ordinary charge. Similarly, the person who pads his or her expense account to any considerable extent suffers no repercussions from the act only because some supervisor is either careless or cooperative.

While most cases can be solved by the application of the general principles developed in the first and second chapters, a few additional warnings should be made. We must distinguish the obligation of an employee or manager—whose position puts him or her in charge of controlling stealing and cheating—from that of the ordinary employee. The person in charge is bound by a work contract as well as by the general obligation not to risk or permit evil. As a result, this person cannot cooperate without violating his or her contract. It is hard to see how the principles covering a proportionate reason for permitting or risking evil can apply in his case. The supervisor who approves what is clearly a dishonest expense account wills the violation of his or her fiduciary relationship. Such a person is not merely risking or permitting the violation.

The employee who is *not* actually in charge of controlling the money or property is in a quite different position. He or she has a general obligation not to risk or permit evil without a proportionate reason but is not bound by a contractual or fiduciary relationship. Thus, the secretary who knows that she is typing up padded expense accounts for her boss may not be able to stop the evil without losing a job that she needs. In this situation, her silence is a form of cooperation, but it is not necessarily unethical.

Active and direct cooperation, in which one actually wills the evil as a means to one's own advancement, is unethical in terms of the general principles we have developed. When a person benefits from the cooperation, we generally have a sign that the cooperation is active and direct and not merely a question of permitting or risking harm for a proportionate reason. This rule of thumb is not infallible and yields to the facts of the case. There are cases where the cooperation yields no monetary reward to the individual but does make that individual feel that he or she has helped a friend. This is unethical even though no money passes hands.

There are cases where a person who is not in charge of preventing the harm may cooperate unwillingly for a proportionate reason. These are difficult cases, and even experts can disagree as to the manner of their resolution. Some, for example, feel that the restaurateur who can stay in business only if he provides sales people with inflated bills has a proportionate reason for cooperating with them. These people reason that the man's livelihood is at stake; that he cannot prevent the evil, and that he does not will or cause the theft but only supplies an instrument of the theft. On the other hand, it is difficult to see how he can be excused, since he lies as a means of staying in business. All would agree, of course, that the restaurateur would be unethical if he offered to cooperate or advertised his willingness through the rumor circuit. In such a case, he would be actively cooperating and perhaps initiating the evil.

Even in those fairly rare cases where persons without a fiduciary relationship might have a proportionate reason for cooperating passively, they still have a duty to work for the correction of the situation. If they refuse to do what they can, they accept the evil and reject alternate solutions.

WHISTLE BLOWING

The discussion of an employee's obligation to mitigate evil goes beyond his or her contractual or general duties to the company. The employee may either know or suspect that either the company, or another employee, or even the president is either endangering the public or cheating customers. Is the employee obliged to blow the whistle on the company or on a supervisor?

In attempting to answer this question, a series of questions must be asked and answered. First, does the employee *know* of the illicit activity or does he or she only *suspect* that something is wrong? Second, is there any founded reason to hope that denunciation of the evil will do any good? Third, does the good justify risking severe retaliation against the whistle blower?

If the employee has only suspicions even after careful investigation, he or she has no obligation to blow the whistle. Indeed, prudence dictates that he or she keep quiet. Both companies and individuals can be unfairly hurt by people who rock the boat on mere suspicion. Suspicions, furthermore, are of little use unless real evidence is forthcoming.

Even if employees have knowledge of an evil, they will have no obligation to blow the whistle unless they can reasonably foresee some good coming from the denunciation. The reason is simple. No one is obliged to do what is useless. The grand gesture and brave but useless gesture may be admirable in some people's eye, but they are not obligatory.

Granted that the employee has knowledge of the evil and some hope of accomplishing a reform, there remains the possibility of savage retaliation. Powerful companies and powerful individuals do not like being denounced and can often get the boat-rocker fired and blackballed. Laws that supposedly protect whistle blowers do not always work. In view of the possibility or rather the probability of retaliation, the whistle blower must decide if the good to be obtained in the concrete outweighs the probability of serious harm to the denouncer. The principle of proportionality is thus back in the center of the stage.

PREVENTATIVE ETHICS

The employer who has the best interests of the company and workers at heart should take steps to minimize the employee's temptation to steal. An adequate company policy is the first step, but it may be useless unless higher management itself follows it. To put it another way, good example is a powerful force in any company.

Temptation can also be reduced if a worker's regular pay is adequate, relative not only to his or her needs, but to the importance of his or her position. Underpaid workers can always justify themselves on the grounds that they are merely taking what is theirs. Good pay thus deprives people of an easy excuse.

Although good policy, good examples, and good pay can solve the problem for most workers, the morally marginal employee will be deterred (though never completely blocked) only by adequate supervision. The regulations of the Internal Revenue Service, which demand proof of expenses beyond certain points, are a great help in maintaining supervision. In addition, the internal auditors should give special attention to expenses that appear to be out of line. The mere fact that such auditing is a regular company policy will at least blunt the larcenous instincts of the potentially immoral employee.

ADDITIONAL CASES AND BASIC PRINCIPLES

Because there is no limit to human ingenuity and the possible situations in business, cases involving honesty and expense accounts could be cited almost indefinitely. Often these cases are presented in a nest of irrelevant detail so that basic issues are confused. Often, too, they come complete with a handy set of justifications from the employee. The honest employee will cut through these excuses and irrelevancies to the basic questions.

1. To whom does the item belong?
2. Is the owner reasonably unwilling that the item pass on to you?
    a. Do I have a clear title to the item?
    b. What is the company policy?
    c. What would my opinion be if roles were reversed?
3. In case of doubt or of unwilling cooperation with others, do I have a proportionate reason for risking or permitting the harm?

Readers may like to work through the following cases on their own. When they are finished, they may look at the questions at the end of the chapter to discover if they have overlooked any important points.

1. John is a wealthy bachelor who works only for pleasure. His employer has not paid his wages for months and refuses to do so. John does not want to bring the case to court because he enjoys working where he is and is too lazy to look for another job. He decides to take his wages by "borrowing" and padding his expense account. "After all," he says, "the wages are due to me." The employer's business is in fair condition, but his cash position is poor since he has just refurnished his offices in modern Danish style and bought a set of expensive oil paintings for the reception rooms.

2. Mary works to support a sick husband and five small children. She gets top wages but is short of money due to heavy medical expenses. She is supposed to control all petty cash and is checked by one other employee who happens to feel sorry for Mary. By cooperating, the two manage to take about $60.00 a week with Mary getting $45.00 of this. Mary feels she has to do this, and her friend agrees for a 25 percent cut.

3. Harry is on an unlimited expense account. He is authorized to write off gambling losses with customers if he puts them down under a variety of headings such as cabs, tips, postage, and so on. Harry pads all of these items even when he has no losses on the grounds that it will look suspicious if he suddenly has to put in fairly large claims for these sums. Besides, he is supposed to lose but can't bear to do so. If he doesn't pad, they will bawl him out for not following orders.

4. Dick has been told by his immediate superior that he is not to check Ms. Johnson's expense accounts. Dick knows that Ms. Johnson is very friendly with his boss and feels that there is something wrong here. The head of the entire operation is an honest man, but Dick does not want to rock the boat, so he remains silent and approves all of Ms. Johnson's accounts. He's only following orders and does not know if this has been approved on higher levels.

QUESTIONS ON CASES

1. Does John have a right to the money? Even if he has a right to the money, does he have a proportionate reason for using this method before he has used the courts?
2. Would Mary's boss be reasonably unwilling for her to take the money if he knew Mary's situation at home? Does Mary's situation have any possible bearing on the actions of her friend?
3. Is Harry cheating the government or forcing the company to do so? Is there commercial bribery involved? Even aside from these questions, does Harry have any possible title to the money?
4. Has Dick neglected an alternate means? Is Dick's feeling pertinent?

BY WAY OF SUMMARY

It is unethical to use company resources except in the implied or expressed interests of the company. Managers have the obligation of preventing such uses, the obligations of other employees to blow the whistle involves problems of proportionality. All employees should remember that with rare exceptions the so-called justifications for taking extra pieces of the pie are only rationalizations for dishonesty.

9

RELATIONS WITH CUSTOMERS: SAFETY AND INFORMATION

INTRODUCTION

The relationship of buyer and seller is crucial in economics, law, and ethics. The way in which we view the relationship, including the rules and institutions we use to govern it, determines in large part the success of the economic system in supplying goods and in supporting the values of society. Some view the relationship as one in which the customer is a pigeon and the seller a villain. Some would like to see the relationship as a mechanical one in which natural forces take care of all ethical problems. Both views are at odds with reality and with the values of our civilization. Granted that the relationship is often impersonal, the fact remains that it is a relationship between human beings who have rights and duties. These rights and duties are the subject of the present chapter and the one that follows.

Since the relationship can take many forms, the present chapter concentrates largely on the obligation of the seller to the ultimate consumer. The first section of the chapter is a rather general examination of the relationship of ultimate sellers, that is to say manufacturers, to consumers and thus to society, regarding product safety and liability. While it is conceded that the range of illustrations contained in the following sections of the chapter is fairly narrow, we maintain that the specific principles developed there coupled with those more general ones discussed in the first part of the chapter can be applied in nearly all but very special buyer-seller situations. In Chapter Twelve, we will have something to say about the special relationship of manufacturers to suppliers and dealers.

SAFETY AND PRODUCT LIABILITY

By traditional standards, business has a clear obligation to take reasonable care that a product will be safe in use. The manufacturer will be liable (that is, responsible) when, in the eyes of society, he fails to do so. What is "reasonable," of course, varies with the nature of the product (some are inherently dangerous), the circumstances of the use, the cost of introducing safety features, and the willingness of people to pay for the extra costs. What we may call "the reasonable care standard" thus leaves a great deal of latitude to business. In practice, however, it can also leave the customer at risk and society exposed to bearing the cost of injured citizens. For this reason, as society started to change its standards of reasonable care and reasonable costs, both the courts and legislatures began imposing greater legal obligations and assigning stricter product safety liability to business. Today there is a struggle between adherents of strict liability and of a modified version of the traditional reasonable care approach. While the authors have their preferences, there is something to be said for each approach.

In its broadest form, the concept of strict liability specifes that a manufacturer can be liable and made to pay damages when a consumer is injured using their product *even though the manufacturer had not acted negligently or was not guilty of wrongful intent.* On the other hand, the modified, traditional view proposes a more limited conception of liability in regard to product safety. It would stipulate, for example, that liability for defective products should be assigned to the manufacturer only when it could be shown that the product was unreasonably dangerous in construction or design, or perhaps only when the manufacturer was perceived as having failed to warn of danger, or when the product did not live up to an express warranty.

An argument in favor of the broadest form of strict liability assumes that, because business has control of design and manufacturing, business can and should be motivated to the highest standards of safety by being forced to follow the highest standard of liability or responsibility. Other standards, it is claimed, do not allow consumers to hold business truly accountable. It has been argued that a consumer with limited means cannot easily prove that the manufacturer was negligent and so must suffer great damage no matter what his ability to pay. Granted that the broad approach lays a greater burden on the business firm, it is not necessarily an unbearable burden, since in most cases the firm can pass on the added costs of safety to all its customers. When this is not possible, the argument holds that society has voted through the market and has thus refused to accept the costs of the product and its dangers.

A second argument for stricter liability on the part of business rests on the idea that consumers have a right to expect safety and protection. Indeed, these expectations are fueled by assurances of safety both expressed and implied by business. Granting, however, that some products are inherently dangerous (chemicals, drugs, power tools), such consumer expectations are reasonable only within limits. The arguments then revolve around the reasonableness of various limits. The modified traditional position attempts to specify those limits by statutory law. Typical attempts to limit liability would make business responsible for injury allegedly caused by a product only when one of the following could be clearly shown:

1. The product was unreasonably dangerous in construction or design.
2. The manufacturer failed to give explicit warning of danger.
3. The product did not live up to an express warranty.

While such an approach makes life easier for business, as noted above, it may leave injured consumers with no real remedy since it is neither easy nor cheap to prove that a manufacturer should have been aware of less dangerous designs, or that the manufacturer's warnings were not inclusive or explicit.

Although narrowing liability may not be completely desirable, a broad concept, which excuses the consumer completely, is equally undesirable. The consumer who misuses the product or who should reasonably have foreseen the consequences of his or her use and took the risk notwithstanding, is at least in part ethically responsible. Legally this contributory negligence should be considered not only in fairness to manufacturers but to prevent the encouragement of reckless behavior by consumers. In short, contributory negligence leads to comparative fault and should lead to a reduction in the damages assessed against manufacturers.

When products are inherently dangerous both user and maker have serious safety obligations. For example, although the user of a chain saw must be aware of and guard against the "kickback phenomenon" as an inherent danger in the product, the manufacturer is still ethically, if not legally, obligated to work aggressively to improve the design and construction of the chain saw in an effort to reduce the incidence of such accidents. At the same time, the customer has an obligation to read and follow directions and even to seek proper instruction in the operation of such dangerous equipment. Perhaps, the users of chain saws should be licensed only after passing a safety test. Certainly a solution of safety problems will involve design, education, and some control of the usage of dangerous products.

While all of the above may seem extremely reasonable, it should not conceal the fact that in a complex technological society life could grind to a halt if we tried to license all use of all dangerous products. Even proper warnings can be difficult when you consider that an accidental mixing of ammonia and chlorine bleach can create toxic chlorine gas. Similarly, the list of warnings about ordinary cold remedies containing caffeine or pseudoephedrine would have to be very long and take up a great deal of space if written in large letters. In short, there is a limit to what warnings can do in reducing dangers connected with product usage.

All the "ifs," "ands," and "buts" connected with both the traditional reasonable care standard and the specific modified version of that standard help to explain why the authors incline to the legal, strict liability standard. We see this as a legal rather than a properly ethical standard. Moreover, we tend to favor it not because business has proven itself irresponsible but rather because in the first place, it provides an insurance plan for injured consumers, and in the second, it hooks into the free market which will decide if the public wants to buy a product where cost, including the cost of insurance, is on the high side.

In the final analysis society and the market used by society must always have the last say about whether business is fulfilling its social function of supplying useful goods and services at a reasonable cost. The social debate as to what constitutes a reasonable cost for product safety continues.

THE FAIR SALES CONTRACT

Sellers must respect not only the health and safety of customers but their freedom and pocketbooks as well. Indeed, our economy depends for its justification not only on its efficiency in producing but on its ability to protect the dignity of buyers. If buyers are exploited, then we have a form of slavery in which one person is used by another no matter what label is placed on the economy. A society that permits sellers the freedom to distribute but denies the consumer true freedom is an economic dictatorship and not part of a democratic system. Historically, it was the existence of such economic slavery that gave rise to communism and socialism. To the extent that such slavery exists today, we can expect the increasing intervention of political power to promote true economic equality. For these reasons, the problem of the fair sales contract is of vital social importance.

Unless sellers recognize buyers as human beings rather than as enemies or as sheep to be shorn, nothing in this chapter or the following one will make much sense. It is only when we accept the dignity of the individual that we can see the ethical necessity of a fair sales contract which respects the rights of both buyer and seller.

A fair sales contract must be a free agreement. Freedom, however, must be based on knowledge. As a result, both *fraud* and *ignorance* can make a contract unfair and so unethical. Freedom also implies that the individual not only has knowledge but is capable of acting on it. A fair contract, then, cannot be the result of *power* which forces people to disregard their own best interests, or of *irrational desires or passion* which cause them to act as if they did not have knowledge.

In view of the nature of the fair sales contract, sellers will be unethical whenever they deliberately *use* fraud or power, or *create* ignorance and passion in order to gain an advantage. In all of these cases, the intent is so clearly wrong that there is little room for dispute about the ethics of such sellers. More often than not, however, the problem is not one of deliberate exploitation but of involvement in a situation where the existing power structure, ignorance, and passion cause the buyers to agree to an unfair contract of sale. We must, then, discuss not only the more obvious unethical acts, but the more subtle obligation to remedy situations which can lead to exploitation.

FRAUD, LYING, AND DECEPTION

Fraud exists when there is a deliberate attempt to deceive someone about a material fact, that is, about a fact that has some importance for the buying decision. It is deliberate deception in a relatively serious area. Lying exists whenever one speaks against one's own mind in circumstances where the other has a reasonable expectation of the truth, whether the matter be serious or not. Deception can result from fraud, lying, ignorance, or negligence, so that its ethical quality depends on more than intent.

Sound ethics condemns *not only the intent* to deceive, when the other has a reasonable expectation of the truth, but also the *risking or permitting of deception* without a proportionate reason. If one can prevent deception by expressing oneself a little more clearly or by eliminating some unnecessary point, which has deceptive implications, one ought to do so. At the same time, there are cases where there is no practical way of preventing the deception of some individuals. Having done one's best, an individual cannot be accused of negligence. Of course, the greater the deception and the harm that may flow from it, the greater effort one must make.

It should be noted that, from an ethical point of view, fraud and lying can exist even though this cannot be established in a court of law. For example, television advertisers who dress announcers in white and place them in a setting which suggests a professional person's study, almost certainly intend to mislead the viewer into believing that their product has a medical endorsement. The deliberately false implication is as unethical as the outright lie even though it may not be as effective in deceiving the public. The same implication might be ethical if it were indeliberate or could not be removed without removing some truthful statement that gave important information about the product.

In dealing with the proportionate reason required to permit or risk deception, it is important to consider the basis for the act and the nature of the audience. Thus, the honest advertiser need not bother him or herself too much when the deception results from the buyer's carelessness in reading properly printed instructions or from his or her wishful thinking. At the same time, the advertiser should realize that the courts, which formerly judged a statement deceptive if it would fool a reasonably prudent person, are beginning to look to the protection of even the gullible and the ignorant. Both ethics and the trend in law, then, would dictate the use of reasonable care in protecting nearly everyone from possible deception.

In attempting to evaluate the deception which might possibly result from a statement or implication, the advertiser should keep his audience in mind. Terms and usage, which may be clear to those in the industry or to professional buyers, can often be confusing to the ordinary consumer. Indeed, we found an executive who had not the slightest idea of the meaning of the promotional terms used by his own salespeople. The confusion of someone about to purchase this person's product must be great. Industry cooperation with the Federal Trade Commission has done much to remedy this problem in some industries, but there are still numerous sectors where the language is clear only to the seller.

Sellers often object to agreeing to standardized terminology and grades which make it easier for the consumer to compare values. To a certain extent their objections are based on the fact that such standardization may make it difficult to promote either marginal differences or real innovations that were not foreseen by the standard maker. Such difficulties are real and should be anticipated. However, they should not cause one to overlook the buyer's need for information. We suspect that often the real objection is not quite so reasonable but rather stems from the fear that standards would enable the consumer to see through the partially fictitious values of branded and heavily advertised goods. If this is the case, then industry may be using its power to prevent the consumer from getting the most for his money.

THE OBLIGATION TO INFORM

The previous paragraphs are largely concerned with the obligation not to deceive and the conditions under which one may ethically permit deception. There remain questions as to when and what a seller must tell the buyer. To put it another way, when and about what is there a positive obligation to inform?

Both ethics and law agree that the seller has an obligation to disclose latent material defects to the buyer if there is to be a valid contract. Except in the case of the genuine as-is sale, the seller does not have a proportionate reason for allowing the buyer to remain in ignorance of such defects. There is, however, a problem as to what constitutes a latent defect in our modern economy. Thus, while a defect is generally considered latent if ordinary inspection will not reveal it, modern packaging and processing often make inspection difficult if not impossible. Moreover, when the buyer is faced with thousands of items in a supermarket, he does not have the time to make even an ordinary inspection. As a result, consumers often find themselves practically unable to get even necessary information. Because the producer and seller are in a position to provide information and because the information is necessary for truly informed buying, we believe that there is an obligation to reveal not only latent defects in the strict sense of the term but many ordinary defects and even positive qualities.

Obviously the right of the consumer to information is not unlimited. If good product information is readily and cheaply available to the user, he or she cannot ask the producer to supply it as a matter of duty. To put it another way, the consumer must take reasonable steps to remedy his or her own ignorance before the producer has an obligation to reveal more than latent substantial defects.

Granted that there is some sort of obligation to reveal more than latent defects and granted the obligation of buyers to do their part in getting information, further precision is necessary though not always possible. The obligation to inform will be particularly strong when the consumer needs the information to avoid serious harm to him or herself. Thus, clear content labeling for nonprescription drugs and prepared foods is obligatory. While these products may be generally safe for use, particular ingredients can be extremely dangerous for many individuals. People with heart problems need to know what soft drinks, reducing pills, pain killers, and cold remedies contain caffeine so that they can follow their physician's order to avoid that ingredient. People with high blood pressure need to know which patent medicines and prepared foods contain sodium and how much sodium. Without such information, they cannot properly follow the diets necessary to preserve their health. Similar obligations can exist with regard to ingredients that are known to cause allergic reactions. Failure to disclose such information is tantamount to indifference to, if not hatred of, one's fellow human beings.

DISCLOSURE IN THE SALE OF CREDIT

There are few areas where full disclosure is more important than in selling credit. Because figures puzzle many people, even compound interest can cause such confusion that people are deceived. When discounts, service charges, and varying methods of repayment are introduced, it takes a determined and sophisticated borrower to ascertain the true cost of the money he or she is buying. Most people never think that the insurance they pay to cover payment of the loan in case of death or disability is a cost. In addition, there is considerable and expensive ignorance about alternate and cheaper sources of credit, with the result that there is more than a little exploitation in our economy.

If anyone thinks this is exaggerated, let them ask their friends and a few fellow workers to compute the true annual percentage cost of money in the following cases.

1. In a revolving credit plan, the customer pays 1.5 percent on the unpaid balance at the end of the month. What true annual interest is being paid for an item bought on June 29, when the customer pays $1.50 interest on June 30 for $100.00?
2. A teacher's credit union charges a contributing member $1.50 interest per month on a loan of $100.00. In figuring, don't forget that the member has some of his own money in the fund from which he is borrowing.

Honest credit agencies do try to disclose the true cost of borrowing. For some reason, however, large groups have fought legislation now in place that requires such disclosure. It almost seems as if they would want to profit from the ignorance of buyers. This opposition to reasonable measures of preventing exploitation is as unethical as the exploitation itself, since it involves the use of power to continue a harmful situation that need not exist to the same degree.

Realistically, it must be admitted that some people cannot be taught or do not want to know the true cost of credit. The obligation, then, is to use reasonable means and not any and all means.

When there is an obligation to reveal defects and positive qualities, this may be done in a variety of ways. In some cases, it is the job of the salesperson; in others, the task falls to labeling and advertising as in the cases of over the counter drugs and nutritional information on certain products. Traditionally, of course, it was salespeople themselves who had the duty of informing the consumer. However, with the growth of impersonal selling through machines and self-service racks, and with the increased number of salespeople who are really only order takers, it would seem more and more necessary to give information on labels and in advertisements, even though these are not technically offers to sell. At the same time, the space and time limits of labels and advertisements reduce the obligations to the consumer, since only the most pertinent information can be given in many cases. Often too, the advertisement is designed to call attention to the existence and availability of the product, so that it cannot be made to bear full responsibility for informing the public.

SOME SPECIAL PROBLEMS IN ADVERTISING

While it would be impossible to give a long list of specific problems and practices in advertising, the material prepared by the Better Business Bureau and the Federal Trade Commission will be both more up-to-date and more detailed than anything given here. Two practices, however, need special comment since they are sometimes confused with legitimate selling tools. In particular, it is necessary to distinguish preticketing from legitimate markdowns, and "bait and switch" advertising from the "loss leader."

Preticketing, or the manufacturer's placing a retail price tag on a product, is legitimate in the abstract. In the concrete, however, it is often a form of cooperation in deceptive pricing and advertising. Some manufacturers use inflated suggested retail prices so that sellers can convince buyers that they are getting a real bargain when the price on the tag is dramatically marked down. The product is not meant to sell at the inflated price, and the preticketing is not meant to inform but to deceive by establishing a fictitious basis of comparison. Such procedures harm not only the consumer but honest competitors; so they are doubly unethical.

The legitimate markdown is a reduction in price based on either the normal or actual selling price in a store or area. It is not deceptive because the basis of comparison is real and not fictitious. Some markdowns are difficult to classify from an ethical point of view except in terms of the seller's intention. A merchant buys some dresses at a particularly low price and wants to sell them as a special. Because this particular merchandise is unfamiliar in his market, he believes customers will not realize what a bargain they are getting unless he displays the markdown. He puts the dresses on sale at what would be their normal price in other markets and in a few days marks them down to the price he actually wanted to charge. Since he does not intend to deceive, but to inform of the true value, we would regard his intention and act as ethical in the absence of laws to the contrary. If his intention had been to deceive as to the normal price, his act would have been unethical.

The "bait and switch" advertiser promotes a fictitious bargain which he does not intend to sell and generally does not stock in any reasonable quantity. He uses the promise of a bargain to bring in the customer whom he then tries to switch to the high priced merchandise he actually intends to move. If the customer insists on the promised bargain, the merchandise sometimes is brought out and discovered to be no bargain at all. More often the buyer is told that the item has already been sold out. Such tactics have been widely used by shady appliance dealers and home improvement companies to the detriment of both consumers and honest competitors. It is false advertising by intent and effect and has done much to harm and lessen public confidence in many retailers.

The "loss leader" is a product sold at a loss in the hope that the customers attracted by a *real* bargain will buy enough other merchandise to yield a good profit. In the absence of laws to the contrary, the "loss leader" is ethical so long as the seller has a reasonable stock or informs the public of the limits of the stock. It is not a deceptive practice, though it can be suspect if other products are given an extra mark-up in order to insure the profit.

Although there are laws in existence that govern sales below cost, conflicts between what is legal and what is ethical may still arise. Resolutions of such conflicts, as always, must tend toward a balancing of the interests of both sellers and buyers, however we feel the burden of responsibility for fairness in such cases rests on the merchant.

IRRATIONAL DESIRE

The critics of business accuse it of encouraging people to live beyond their means. Some business people, affected by these charges, suffer pangs of conscience when they see people buying things they cannot afford. So long as the business person has not deliberately encouraged buyers to act irrationally, he or she need only make reasonable efforts to help the customer act intelligently. In most cases these efforts would amount to no more than pointing out those elements of the situation that the customer may have overlooked. Often indeed, there is nothing to be done, since people resent meddling even when they are not deaf to unpleasant facts. There are cases, however, where stronger action may be required.

Funeral directors are generally dealing with people whose emotions make them incapable of rational choice. Guilt-ridden, hypnotized by the awful present, the survivors will often neglect their own future. Their inability to cope with facts, figures, and the future makes them profitable customers for the "friendly" mortician. Here is a case where the funeral director must look not only to his or her pocketbook but to the needs of the living. If such a mortician does not, he or she can be *a* cause, if not the cause, for leaving a grieving spouse with nothing but receipted funeral bills.

Similar situations arise with the young couple buying an engagement ring, parents arranging a wedding, and people borrowing money to pay for medical expenses. To a lesser extent, many salespeople exploit the emotions of parents in peddling encyclopedias to people who cannot afford them. We have all heard stories of encyclopedias being "placed" in the homes of poor people who could neither speak nor read English. It is difficult to label this as anything but exploitation of ignorance and passion. While the business person is not the financial advisor of such people, he or she must still take reasonable measures to make sure that he or she does not exploit emotion and irrational desire.

The extreme cases given above should not be taken to imply a condemnation of emotion.[1] Our feelings can support us and help us to focus our attention. Sellers and advertisers can use emotion to help consumers. What we are condemning is the exploitation of people whose emotions, uncontrolled by reason, cause them to act irrationally.

Our examples are drawn from personal selling rather than from advertising, since the real crisis exists in the realm of face-to-face contacts. It can, of course, be argued that advertising itself is probably a marginal factor in producing irrational behavior based on emotion.[2] To be sure, the intention to exploit through appeal to emotions is unethical, but the harmful effects of much advertising can be offset by the good effects when the advertiser is not seeking to distract from the objective facts.

PUBLICITY AND PUBLIC RELATIONS

The shared responsibility of producer, agent, and media is nowhere so apparent as in publicity and public relations. While an advertisement is a paid announce-

[1]See Thomas M. Garrett, *An Introduction to Some Ethical Problems of Modern American Advertising* (Rome, Italy: Gregorian University Press, 1961), pp. 37–52.

[2]Ibid., pp. 95–132. It is perhaps not really necessary to point out that subliminal advertising is both illegal and unethical. However, on the more complex issue as to whether or not continuous exposure to advertisements which attempt to persuade primarily by emotion or desire can serve to dispose us in the long run to adopt base values (eg. consumption for its own sake), see Stanley Benn "Freedom and Persuasion," in *Ethical Theory and Business,* 2nd ed. eds., Tom L. Beauchamp and Norman E. Bowie (Englewood Cliffs, NJ: Prentice Hall, Inc. 1983), pp. 367–376. See, of course, on the influence of advertising on free and rational choice John Kenneth Galbraith's "dependence effect" argument in *The Affluent Society,* 3rd ed., revised by John Kenneth Galbraith. Copyright 1958, 1969, 1976 by John Kenneth Galbraith, Houghton Mifflin Co. For a response to this argument see F. A. Von Hayek, "The Non Sequitur of the 'Dependence Effect'," *Southern Economic Journal,* 27 (1961), 346–348.

ment and recognizable as such, publicity and public relations stories appear as unbiased editorial material. For this reason, all who are involved in processing or publishing such releases must be extremely careful. This is especially true in financial public relations where a lie or a false implication can cause serious financial harm. No financial editor wants to find him or herself touting stocks on the unexamined information of a public relations department, nor does a reputable P.R. person wish to be duped by some unscrupulous executive. Wishes are not enough protection, however, and competent checking is in order.

Product publicity, which appears in the shopper's guide, poses the same sort of problems. Often there can be potential conflicts of interest when a hungry advertising department pressures the editorial people to do them a favor by giving a free "plug" to an advertiser. The editorial department needs to be insulated from such pressure and indoctrinated with the idea that it must guard the consumer rather than the ad salesperson's commissions.

The shared responsibility of many agents in the advertising, public relations, and publicity processes points up a more general problem in business ethics. Whenever responsibility is not assigned with some precision, it tends to evaporate into a cloud of excuses. In such a cloud, not only self-regulation, but any regulation becomes an impossibility or, at best, an accidental occurrence. Good ethics demands that such situations be avoided, since they are a breeding ground for unethical or at least irresponsible conduct. In the case of advertising and public relations, it should be made clear that although one person must ultimately take the praise or blame, each agent is responsible for reporting errors he or she may detect. Moreover, it is generally necessary to specify who must check for accuracy when copy is passed from one independent group to another. The television networks, for example, make their own check of medical claims made by advertisers and have located the responsibility clearly in their Continuity Acceptance Departments. The other media and local stations would do well to imitate them in this, although, of course, their resources are more limited.

PACKAGING AND LABELING

A package has numerous functions. It protects the product in transit and in storage, facilitates use, provides information about the contents, and in many cases, serves as an advertising medium. Unfortunately, a package can be defective in the performance of any one of these functions and may even be used to deceive consumers.

Most of the ethical problems, however, do not involve the use of packaging for outright deception but the failure of the package to give adequate information. In most cases, the problem is closely connected with the manner and method of advertising itself.

There is the problem of the "large economy size" that actually costs more per ounce than the regular size, the "cents-off" sale in which no information is given about the regular price, the use of odd ounces, the reduction of contents without reducing package size, the slack fill, and the use of small type for essential information. Most of these problems can be solved by asking the following questions based on our principles.

1. Is the package intended to deceive or exploit?
2. If there is no intention to deceive, is there a proportionate reason for permitting or risking deception?

Proportionate reasons may exist in this area when one function of the package demands that another function be neglected in part. The slack fill is often a result not of the intention to deceive, but of the nature of the product itself which causes it to settle in transit. A small package may demand small type. Providing a handle on a bottle may produce a shape that does not reflect the true contents or size. The utility of having a standard package size in a given line may justify the odd ounce content, since obviously space is not directly related to weight.

On the other hand, there are many practices that are actually deceptive, no matter what the intentions of the packer. There can be absolutely no excuse for calling a package a "large economy size" when it actually costs more per ounce than the regular size. It is difficult to imagine any proportionate reason for the introduction of such descriptive terms as "tall," or "giant." Such terminology is either misleading or meaningless. It is hard to see anything but deception when a roll-on deodorant in a plastic container is put in a box twice as large as is required. It is difficult to see any justification for using small print and poor contrasting backgrounds on a package that has plenty of room for the senseless illustration which is already on it.

Possibly the most potentially deceptive practices are found where a packager reduces the contents without giving any prominence to the statement of contents. The danger is compounded when the package is then labeled "25¢ off," although the new price per ounce is actually higher than the old one. Of course the consumer might be able to detect a number of these frauds if he were to shop with a slide rule, a computer, and a photographic memory in which had been recorded all previous prices.

One answer to many of these difficulties is that American packers should move aggressively toward more uniform regulations and standards for packaging. While we believe that great care is needed in setting up standard definitions of allotments and standard package sizes for everything, we feel that it is possible to work out flexible standards on fill and change of weight and content.

There are considerable advantages for both business and consumers in such a move toward more strict standardization of packaging. Individual companies might, for example, standardize their own packages in such a way as to make maximum use of shelf space, warehouses, and trucking. The results would be increased profits along with lower prices to consumers. Also, large scale standardization throughout the packaging industry would help eliminate some difficulties with trade in the international market, wherein numbers of nations do have standardization packaging.

There are of course some problems in imposing uniform packaging standards on business. As is often the case with strict regulations, the costs of meeting them could be high for business if, for example, significant retooling or changes in technology in their plants were necessary. This might entail increased cost for the consumer as well, at least in the short run. Also, larger firms would be able to absorb added costs more easily than smaller ones.

Granting the above mentioned difficulties, which demand caution, in our judgment cooperation on the part of business in encouraging more uniform packaging standards will improve the efficiency of our distribution sector and will serve to help protect consumers by eliminating many doubtful practices—for example, ambiguous statements about content and weight, deceptive color contrasts, and unclear or microscopic type—for which there is no reasonable excuse.

THE ETHICS OF BUYERS

The ethics of buyers is to a large extent the reverse side of the ethics of sellers. The buyer too must not exploit by fraud or power or passion. The position of the buyer with regard to ignorance, however, is slightly different from that of the seller. The seller must disclose substantial defects to the buyer, but with a few exceptions, the buyer does not have to reveal hidden virtues to the seller. The assumption is that the seller, having the property in his own hands, should know its worth.

While sellers must disclose substantial defects, this does not excuse buyers from gathering information and comparing products. The buyer, after all, has an obligation to use his resources intelligently. Often, indeed, it is the careless buyer who has made it possible for the dishonest seller to deceive and exploit ignorance. Industrial buyers who are skilled can help to improve economic performance, but lazy consumers who buy without information can encourage the substitution of tricks for real value. The shrewder buyers become, the easier it will be to enforce honesty in the marketplace. If buyers are skilled, honesty will not only be good ethics but the best road to profits.

There are a few cases where the buyer, being also the appraiser, may be obliged to reveal hidden values to the seller. The jeweler who is asked the worth of a diamond by an owner who wishes to sell, should either suggest a separate appraisal or state the true value in trade at that level. If the jeweler answers by making an offer well below true value, he may be using his role as an appraiser to help himself to an unfair profit in his role as buyer.

BY WAY OF SUMMARY

Sellers are unethical whenever they intend to exploit whether they cause the deception, ignorance, and passion, or deliberately set out to take advantage of it. In other cases, where sellers are not the cause of the buyer's disability and do not intend to take advantage of it, they may proceed if they cannot change the situation by reasonable means.

In the following chapter, we shall meet problems involving the use of power to exploit. In Chapter Eleven, we shall consider some side effects of unethical exploitation of consumers, and in Chapter Twelve, we shall return to study relationships of dealers and suppliers.

10

RELATIONS WITH CUSTOMERS: PRICES

INTRODUCTION

Prices and the price level affect the welfare of sellers, buyers, and competitors as well as the functioning of the competitive system and the economy. As a result, the fairness of prices is a central issue in business ethics as it is in law and economics. At the same time, it is a difficult question for which there is at present no completely satisfactory answer in either theory or practice. At times, pricing practices give the appearance of competition but in reality only protect sellers at the expense of consumers. Prices that are most beneficial to consumers and individual sellers can lead to economic concentration and possible government control. Laws designed to protect small dealers can and do raise prices and subsidize inefficiency. Indeed, the laws often encourage pricing that reduces efficiency and robs the economy of even the limited benefits of competition.

In many cases, it is nearly impossible to evaluate the long-range effects of prices, for our economy is so dynamic and complex that uncertainty can be high. The variety of buyer-seller relations makes generalizations especially dangerous. Existing theory can further confuse our perception of the reality of pricing, for it often rests on false assumptions. It is no wonder, then, that business people are uneasy, critics outraged, and students of ethics frankly puzzled. We are indeed in much the same position as we were when treating wages; convinced that there is a norm, we are unable to pin it down with satisfactory clarity. Once again, then, we shall proced cautiously, pointing out obvious abuses and giving some broad rules that will at least narrow the gray areas.

DIFFICULTIES WITH EXISTING THEORIES

Older theories of the ethics of pricing suffer from two defects; they are inapplicable to many segments of the American economy, and they make no allowance for the cost of price instability. These defects arise from the fact that both our economic and ethical theory were developed to explain or regulate a much simpler economy. Even though these older theories may not be very useful today, a brief consideration of them will help to illustrate the problems involved in any theory of fair pricing.

In simpler economies, characterized by near perfect competition, prices were set by the *collective judgment* of a fairly large number of buyers and sellers. So long as there was real freedom, it could be assumed that the resulting price or rather range of prices was fair, since it represented a community judgment of the *exchange value* of the goods in question. Resources were also allocated in accord with the value judgments of the community, since the prices tended to equalize supply and demand. In this way, both individual justice and the social good were served. It was with such a market in mind that medieval writers and their followers equated the fair price with the free-market price. The price or *price range* so established was binding on both buyers and sellers unless some particular circumstance (though never the need of the individual buyer), justified a lowering or raising of the price.

This theory, which corresponds closely to the classical economic model of price formation, is inapplicable to large segments of our economy, since the market is not perfect, and large buyers and sellers are often in a position to set the price unilaterally within broad limits. Buyers, moreover, often lack the information necessary to form correct judgments of exchange value. The problem arises from the fact that the present market does not equalize the power of buyers and sellers but tends in many cases to build up power blocks that can call the tune. For all of these reasons, the theory that equates the fair price with the free-market price is not too useful in an economy where many markets are not truly free.

Some might assume that we could change the economy in such a way that free markets and fair prices would prevail once again. This change would not only be impossible but might not produce the desired social results. While true price competition certainly gives consumers lower prices and the economy fair prices, it also tends to produce instability, which makes it difficult to plan research, innovations, and future markets. It is for this reason that many companies avoid price competition and seek to administer prices in the interest of stability and planned growth. It is for the same reason that governments have frequently intervened to fix prices either directly or indirectly. In short, the cost of the perfect market may be too high for the good of society and for large groups of individuals. To put it another way, the prices set by perfect competition may not maximize even economic welfare in the long run.

It should be noted in this context that price instability can be particularly hard on individuals and institutions that depend for their income on savings, investments, and pensions with a fixed value but not a fixed purchasing power. Moreover, although drops in prices may benefit the poor, raises can be disasterous for many groups. A glance at the curse of the depression or runaway inflation will confirm most of these statements.

DIFFICULTIES WITH THE LAW

Even if business people wanted to engage in real price competition, the law would often prevent them, or at least moderate their enthusiasm, if their efforts proved profitable. If General Motors priced its products to assure the maximum total profit, it would so undercut its competitors that there would soon not be even the semblance of competition. At this point, General Motors would find itself faced with an anti-trust suit. As a result, General Motors, like so many leaders in fields where there are few competitors, finds it safer, if not more profitable, to hold back and permit other companies to stay in business. This provides us with the appearance of competition but not with its classical virtues. It also gives us a set of administered prices and an ethical problem.

The Robinson-Patman Act, Fair Trade Laws (which are actually resale price maintenance laws), and the laws on sales below cost can reduce competition while preserving the appearance of it. We are, then, faced with a paradox. The laws, which should bring the benefits of competition in price to the consumer, actually discourage price competition. Indeed, the final result may be the creation of a situation in which business people cannot enter into truly fair contracts of sale even if they desire to do so. In any event, the law often creates proportionate reasons for risking or permitting the undesirable effects of many pricing practices.

PRICING PRACTICES AND PROBLEMS

Because power is a fact and the law encourages it indirectly, prices are not set by competition in large segments of the economy. More often than not, they do not result from a free interchange between buyers and sellers, but are set in a variety of ways and in view of a variety of goals. This is true not only of the prices of commodities and finished products but of labor. To a certain extent, it must be this way. The new product has to be offered at some price, and if there are no substitutes, the seller may have wide latitude since buyers, having little basis of comparison, may be willing to accept it. Moreover, many businesses can survive only if they charge for future costs and future services in the price of products they are selling here and now. This, of course, brings in the whole problem of capital formation in the modern American economy. It raises questions not only of the fairness of prices but of social utility when private groups such as the modern corporation are allowed to be major instruments of capital formation through their ability to exact a sort of *forced savings* from the customer.

A VERY TENTATIVE THEORY

Our remarks thus far should indicate the difficulty of evolving a modern ethic of pricing adequate to the economy as it exists. Indeed, we do not believe that our understanding of the economy and its relationship with the political order is great enough to permit the development of an adequate theory at this time. In the meantime, it is suggested that a rough judgment of the fairness of prices can be made in terms of the four factors that can vitiate the fair sales contract; *fraud, ignorance, power, and passion.* As in the past chapter, allowances must be made for the existence of proportionate reasons for permitting the unwilled effects of some acts and situations that cannot be easily changed. This, of course, leaves many of the broader social questions untouched. We shall, however, return to them in our chapter on the relationship of business to the social economy.

PRICE FIXING

Conspiratorial price fixing is condemned not only by the law but by ethics. The reason is that the *conspiracy causes power to destroy equality between buyer and seller.* Furthermore, it involves a type of fraud since the buyer is led to believe that he or she is dealing with independent offers. When the price fixing results in actual losses to the buyer, we are, in addition, dealing with a type of theft or at least unjustified damnification. Finally, conspiratorial price fixing interferes with the economic mechanism that is supposed to govern the pricing and distribution of products.

Conspiratorial price fixing tends to exist in industries with certain common characteristics: overcapacity, special buyer specifications, and buyer power—at least to postpone purchases, if not to demand price concessions. In such industries, real price competition can destroy or cripple smaller and less efficient operators just as it is supposed to do in classical theory. Unfortunately, real price competition can also lead to antitrust prosecution of the survivor and to waste of resources, which are sunk costs and cannot easily be applied to other uses. Strong producers and even society thus have some interest in protecting marginal producers. Conspiracy is, nevertheless, both an unethical and an illegal method of attaining this goal. Furthermore, because inefficiency is protected, the whole of society has an interest in deciding how the situation should be remedied. When private groups decide, they are really unsurping authority that society has not given to them.

PRICE LEADERSHIP

Price leadership occurs when a dominant producer changes its prices and all or most competitors follow the leader. Legally, price leadership is not the same as price fixing. The effects, however, are often identical. In particular, power makes customers pay more than they would in a truly free market. This means that they are "taxed" to assure the continued existence of marginal firms as well as to increase profits of efficient producers. The evil of price leadership, moreover, generally results from the fear that the leader will use its power to retaliate against those who dare engage in price competition. Once again, it is power that causes the destruction of true economic freedom for both producer and consumer.

Given the actual situation in many industries, it is difficult to accuse either price leaders or followers of unethical conduct without qualification. Does a particular company have any real choice about following or leading? Even if it has a choice, can it exercise it without inviting retaliation from either competitors or the government? The answer to these questions will sometimes indicate that a producer may have little or no freedom to change the existing practices. In short, there comes a point where it is the entire complex, rather than the isolated acts of individuals, that creates exploitation through power. When this is the case, a producer who does not intend to produce these effects may permit them for a proportionate reason. Often the reason is simply that he or she can do nothing to provide an immediate remedy. However, the producer must recognize the existence of an obligation to work for a remedy in the long run.

When such situations exist, justice, or at least an approximation of it, can be restored only by society as a whole. There is a price to pay for government intervention, but the price must be weighed against the costs already being incurred. This is not the place to settle the issue, but it should be clear that the solution will not be found in slogans but only in careful research and the imaginative development of new economic systems. While no solution will ever be perfect, we must admit that we have been fairly successful in devising systems that regulate utilities in the interests of consumers while preserving many of the benefits of private enterprise. Perhaps, the scale necessary for many industries will indicate that time is creating new natural monopolies that cannot and should not be controlled by the market, but by the society as a whole.

THE ADMINISTERED PRICE

We must face the fact that producers do not want price competition in many cases. Price competition disciplines the inefficient and limits management's freedom to plan for the future. As a result, the administered price is an ideal that firms would like to make a reality, since it gives them more freedom and greater stability. While the administered price takes several forms, at base it is a price set by producers and sellers rather than by the forces of short run supply and demand. The price, usually decided by the principal producer or supplier in a given line, is more stable than prices set by supply and demand, so that planning is more feasible. Moreover, since it is generally followed by competitors, buyers have little choice. It is not a monopoly price since both competitive forces and the fear of government are always present to some extent. However, many firms are well enough insulated against the full impact of a free market to control their profits and prices within fairly broad limits. The result is that consumers often pay more for the product than they would have in a free market. Sometimes, however, they pay less since the administered price does not automatically go up in some situations.

Even in those cases where the consumer pays more it is not easy to condemn the administrative price without qualification. Some firms use the extra margin of profit for research and expansion. It may be argued that the consumer pays less in the long-run. In addition part of the price may be considered an investment by the consumer in the future of the economy. While such investment is certainly a social necessity, we may ask whether or not it is healthy for private firms to have so much say about the allocation of resources against the future. In point of fact, they actually have the power to tax or to force savings that is ordinarily reserved to the government. Furthermore, because they are at least partially free from the competitive pressure of the financial market, they are no longer completely responsible to even this limited social control of resources. We are then faced with a problem that deserves serious study from both an economic and ethical point of view.

While this is not the place to discuss the full social and political significance of administered prices, the business person should not dismiss the problem lightly.[1] Administered prices allow many companies to accumulate capital, power, and the possibility of controlling larger and larger areas of the economy, not by virtue of real productive and distributive efficiency, but because of their financial position. Sooner or later the existence of such power, which is not directly controlled by society, will call forth more and more government regulation. This day can be postponed by public relations and lobbying, but in the long run, society cannot permit large private power centers that are not responsible to the best interests of society. If the market no longer demands accountability and no longer enforces the discipline that promotes fairness by equalizing power, some other agency will be found.

We do not believe public opinion can do the job completely, for public opinion is not an entirely independent or directed force. Neither do we put much faith in the theory of countervailing power, which entails one giant holding another in check. Power can neutralize power selectively so that the powerless and the unorganized—consumers, for example—are still exploited.

[1]Gardiner C. Means, *The Corporate Revolution in America: Economic Reality* vs. *Economic Theory* (Crowell-Collier, 1962), provides very clear insight into the significance of the administered price.

Because of the legal situation and the actual structure of industries, society as well as business must bear the blame for the situation. Unfortunately, law and existing systems are not easily changed so that the obligation is not to cease administering prices at once, but rather to seek a solution in which all interested parties play a part.

Actually, an adequate solution is impossible except within the larger framework of the American economy. Companies with administered prices often pay the best wages because they are able to do so. Pure price competition may rob us of this benefit, yet there is the suspicion that these adequate wages result from a power struggle between big companies and big unions in which the consumer ultimately pays the bill. We cannot, then, attain the power balance necessary for a just society without considering the power of unions as well as that of corporations.

RESALE PRICE MAINTENANCE

While our laws forbid horizontal price fixing (that between competitors), they have sometimes permitted or even encouraged vertical price fixing (that between producers and their dealers). One form of vertical price fixing can be called Resale Price Maintenance. This is a procedure by which the producer controls the retail price. Retailers are forbidden to sell below the price set by the manufacturer, and this has, in the past, been enforced by law. While the laws that authorized such arrangements were given such euphemistic labels as "fair trade laws" and "quality stabilization laws," they served to reduce price competition and force higher prices on consumers. Like conspiratorial horizontal price fixing, resale price maintenance practices also served to protect marginal and inefficient economic units by guaranteeing them higher margins of profit than they could obtain in real competition.

Obviously someone benefits from resale price maintenance, but the question is whether the benefits offset the losses and whether the benefits are gained by unethical means.

The manufacturer of branded items wants resale price maintenance to protect his or her product image from erosion resulting from its use as a "loss leader" or as a heavily discounted item. If one or more merchants continually sells his or her products with a low mark-up, the manufacturer fears that customers will refuse to pay more. Retailers who face this type of competition are liable to follow suit and ask the manufacturer to reduce his price. When large discounters are in the field, the manufacturer has to deal with several powerful buyers who can hurt him or her or at least reduce his or her freedom. All in all, then, resale price maintenance helps the manufacturer find shelter from some of the forces of the market. A manufacturer's desire to do so is understandable given that large sums of money have been spent on advertising and branding. The manufacturer's actions, however, may not improve the performance of the economy and the lot of the consumer in any significant way.

Resale price maintenance protects the dealer from competition. However, it also restricts those who consider their profit a result of volume rather than of a high mark-up. This means that the consumer cannot benefit from all the economics of scale in selling. Further, by discouraging low price and volume selling, resale price maintenance protects dealers who, for one reason or another, have not reached or do not want to reach the most efficient scale of operations. The manufacturer is not unhappy about this since his or her channels of distribution are protected, but the consumer must pay more.

Sometimes it is argued that price margins must be kept high in order to insure service. Consumers, however, do not always want to buy service, and resale price maintenance forces them to purchase more of a package than they desire. Here is the use of power to force prices up, or at least to make consumers buy more than they want. This, in our opinion, is unethical.

Even when the power of the government was used to enforce resale price maintenance, the practice was wrong for the government was protecting the interests of one private group at the expense of another private group in circumstances where this is not necessary for the public good. Indeed, it is against the public good, insofar as this is generally understood, to include creating the maximum freedom in business consistent with good order in society as a whole.

Fortunately, large retailers and discounters had an interest in removing resale price maintenance laws from the books so that, in many cases, the public has had some freedom of choice. Others, however, continue to seek the passage and enforcement of those laws that tax the consumer without returning proportionate benefits to the society as a whole. This group, it seems, believes in freedom for producers but not for buyers and sellers who want to serve those customers interested in price.

PRICE AND ADVERTISING

False and misleading advertising certainly leads to unfair prices, since the customer pays more than he would have if he had known the truth about the product. This is one of the major reasons for condemning false advertising as unethical. Even technically honest advertising can create illusions, which lead the consumer to pay more than he should. This is not the fault of the advertiser alone but of careless buyers who identify the branded and advertised item with quality and sometimes even use price as an index of quality. In most cases, of course, advertised and branded products are of good quality, readily available, and carefully controlled. Price differentials, however, reflect more than the costs needed to provide these services. Thus, a physician who prescribes drugs by their generic name rather than by brand name saves his patient a bit of money. The shopper who buys private unadvertised labels of the great merchandising chains such as Penney's can often get superior merchandise at prices below those of advertised brands of similar quality. Often, the private label is made by the same company to the same specifications, the difference being in the buyer's illusion rather than in any quality of the goods. Each case, however, should be considered on its own merits, since facts take precedence over theory. When the facts are known, the principles can be applied.

It is difficult to draw the line between true value and actual price. It is also nearly impossible to conceive of a method by which even the most scrupulous advertiser can avoid creating some illusion. So long as buyers are careless, there is little an advertiser can do. As long as competition takes the form of advertising and nonprice differentation, it would be suicide for many manufacturers to change their tactics. In addition, it must be admitted that even if all buyers were very efficient, we would still need advertising to inform and persuade rationally. In view of this, it seems to us that the real ethical problem arises when producers and retailers use fraud and power to prevent those who want price differences from enjoying them. In particular, the use of resale price maintenance laws appear unjust in this context.

The above paragraphs are not to be taken as an approval of the deliberate attempt to get higher prices by creating an illusion. They are, rather, a recognition of the limits of the producer's power to avoid harm and of the proportionate reasons for permitting what is almost inevitable in a society composed of fallible human beings. Once again, the ethics of the business person are enmeshed in the whole web of human society so that it cannot be governed by an ethic designed for angels.

PRICE AND PASSION

An unjust price can result not only from fraud and power but from passion and irrational desire, which can destroy or limit freedom. The most obvious example, as mentioned previously in Chapter Nine, is that of the case of the funeral director who can sell the bereaved almost anything at any price because emotions have robbed this individual of rationality and control. There are times, of course, when even the honest funeral director cannot dissuade the survivors from a foolish act, but there would seem to be no excuse for charging inflated prices no matter how foolish the customer.

Something similar can be said of loan companies who are dealing with people either in dire straits or so hypnotized by desire that they lose all sense of proportion. We do not mean that the business person is the customer's conscience, but he or she does have an obligation to use reasonable means to prevent other human beings from harming themselves. In the case of the loan company, this at least involves some effort to inform the customer about the true price of the money being borrowed.

In recent times, advertisers and sellers have been accused not merely of exploiting existing passion but of creating it for their own purposes. The intention to create an irrational passion, which can be exploited, is objectively unethical. However, it is very difficult to say whether or not sellers can create this passion with any ease or consistency. Thus, advertising, for all its effectiveness, is only a marginal force in creating demand. Furthermore, in a great many cases, its effect on demand increases rather than decreases rationality. As a result, each case is to be examined on its own merits rather than included in a blanket condemnation of persuasive advertising. Where there is no intention to create and exploit irrational desire, the seller's obligation is only to take reasonable steps to protect the customer from stupidity.

While there may not be a great many cases where passion is either created or exploited, these do exist and should not be overlooked. The ticket scalper and the person who initiates scare buying are both in this class. Their price and their profit are not a result of fair exchange, but of exploited inequality. Actually, there are two evils here: the harm to rationality, and the unnecessary dent in the customer's pocketbook.

In certain areas, price is so much higher than cost, even though one is dealing with volume sales, that passion, power, and fraud all seem to be involved. In particular, this is true of toiletries and proprietary drugs. In these cases, unfortunately, much of the difficulty is the fault of the consumer who wants to be fooled or is so emotionally involved that he or she refuses to think clearly. In short, the customer is a sitting duck asking to be shot and then seemingly enjoying it. For example, there are people who take price as a certain sign of quality and will not buy the less expensive item even when it is the best available. As a result, sellers resort to double and triple pricing for the same product, since only thus can they cover all segments of the market. Although this situation results in people paying more for the product than it is worth, it is difficult to condemn the individual seller. However, the cumulative effects of this may cause serious misallocation of resources in society so that the situation itself is an evil. Whether or not this calls for legislation, that is, control by society as a whole, will depend on the severity of the harm. We must face the fact that every society must tolerate some evils lest the remedy be worse than the disease.

DISCRIMINATORY PRICING

As we saw in the chapter on hiring and firing, discrimination is unethical only when based on factors that are not relevant to job qualifications. The case of discrimination in pricing is similar but more difficult, since it is not always clear what factors are relevant in pricing. In addition, discriminatory and unethical pricing injures not only buyers but competitors as well. Finally, it can even be difficult to determine what constitutes the mere fact of a price difference, since there are a vast variety of discounts, allowances, fees, services, and premiums that certainly affect the cost to the buyer. A trade-in allowance may be a real reduction in price, but under some circumstances, it can conceal a price increase. Discounts given to employees may be actual reductions in price or increases in wages depending on one's point of view. Rather than become involved in unnecessary subtlety, we shall treat price as the actual money cost to the buyer and allow disputed points to be settled by the conscience of the agents involved.

Everyone will agree that the cost of manufacturing for shipping to and servicing a buyer is relevant to price differentials. All other things being equal, it costs less to process and ship large orders. A seller is not discriminating against those who buy in small lots when he or she passes on part of the savings to a big buyer so long as the reduction is available to all who can meet the cost-related conditions. At the same time, so long as the price is fair, there is nothing in ethics or law which forces the seller to pass on all or part of the economies of scale.

The cost justification of price differentials is unfortunately complicated by the Robinson-Patman Act and its enforcement. Many of the problems arise from the fact that the seller must justify his reductions. This is easier said than done, for costing is neither an exact science nor an art whose rules are accepted by everyone. As Fennelly has pointed out, the business person may use one method of justification while lawyers and the courts use another.[2] The result is that it is often difficult to tell when one is violating the law even if a particular price is completely ethical in the abstract.

Because it is difficult to assign costs, sound ethics demand not mathematical precision but an honest effort. At best, even the most honest business person can only make a rough estimate. Although the government has, on occasion, tried to establish the costs of a given sale down to the third decimal place, such an approach seems futile. Accounting is not set up to give the actual cost of a particular sale. Both business and accounting are rightfully more concerned with average unit costs rather than with the exact costs of doing business with an individual customer.

Although the law may not always recognize them as legal, discounts given to promote good will or win word of mouth advertising appear to be ethical even though the precise benefit to the seller cannot be calculated. In this class are discounts to professors, clergymen, and others whose opinion is highly respected. Discounts to employees, if not treated as part of their wages, may also fall into this classification. If nothing else, custom would seem to tolerate these differentials.

Other discriminations have traditionally been justified on the basis of the buyer's need rather than on the seller's cost or advantage. Discounts to charitable institutions and some nonprofit organizations are generally acceptable, probably because the recipients are not in competition and thus not subject to our ideas of the ordinary commercial relationship.

Both laws and ethics recognize the legitimacy of price differentials needed to meet competition. Once again, however, the law's requirements are such that honest businessmen cannot always tell when they are acting legally. This excep-

[2]Donald J. Fennelly, "On the Judging of Mince Pies," *Harvard Business Review,* Vol. 42 (November-December, 1964), p. 82.

tion merely recognizes the fact that the seller can in the face of competition have some proportionate reason for risking or permitting harm to the competitors of those who get a more favorable price.

Functional discounts paid to a buyer who performs a service for the seller, such as warehousing or brokering, are also ethical and legal since they really reflect a cost differential to the seller. Problems arise, however, when it comes to determining the size of the discount, since it is difficult to cost these services.

Not only the seller but the buyer is bound by the ethics of price discrimination. Big buyers are often in a position to extort concessions that are not related to their own efficiency or to the cost savings realized by the seller. Often, too, the seller wants to give price concessions to big buyers. The reason, underlying all volume selling, is that a smaller unit profit means little if volume gives a much greater total profit. Indeed, if a seller has unused capacity or idle equipment, a discount that wipes out all unit profit but helps the seller to cover overhead and fixed costs may be very good business. Whether the concession is extorted or given freely because it is truly profitable for the seller, it can hurt the competitors of both the buyer and the seller. If the hurt results from objective factors such as efficiency or cost savings to the seller, then there is nothing unethical about it.

Since the profit of the seller is not necessarily an indication of cost savings, it is not a justification for discrimination in itself. Both law and ethics permit discrimination when it is necessary to meet *bona fide* prices of competitors, but once again, the interpretation of the law makes it difficult to defend oneself on this ground.

As we have noted several times, the Robinson-Patman Act complicates ethics at this point, since it makes it difficult, even impossible, to defend an action for price discrimination. Indeed, it often leaves business people in doubt as to whether or not they are violating the law. Some refer to this as the law that it is impossible to obey. Others say it is not a question of obeying the law, but of deciding which of its provisions you will break since you cannot simultaneously observe all even with the best good will in the world. In the concrete, the law, which was designed to prevent real abuses, has often led to an abandonment of price competition, since this has become almost inherently dangerous. As a result, the law may protect competitors, but it may actually lead to consumers' paying more. We would venture the opinion that there is need for much reworking of our legislation in this area.

PRICING AND INFLATION

As already noted, inflation hurts those on fixed incomes and favors many who are in debt, since inflation allows them to pay off their debts in deflated currency. Serious inflation causes dislocations in the total economy and can create serious problems in international trade. Inflation can discourage savings because savings just disappear as purchasing power diminishes. This effect on savings, then, inhibits capital formation and the ability of financial institutions to provide capital at reasonable costs. In general, anything more than a nominal inflation is a social evil. Assigning responsibility for the evil is, unfortunately, not a simple task.

While business may be assigned some of the blame for inflation, unions, consumers, and the government are just as frequently guilty parties. The propagandists for each group try to lay the blame on the others. Even though economists take sides, the fact remains that everyone contributes to the creation of the problem in the hope that they will not end up as a victim. Unions demand more money, in part because of the desire for more, in part because the cost of living is increasing or is seen to be increasing. Business raises prices in part to cover increased costs of labor, material, and capital but, also, in anticipation of increased costs. Government can cause inflation by borrowing to cover deficits thus decreasing the supply of capital, and increasing its costs. Although consumers are generally seen as the victims *par excellence,* they too are guilty in many instances. Consumers who individually or collectively refuse to resist price increase must share the blame. Perhaps all those who have forgotten the old adage, "Make, make do, and do without," have created a world of very expensive indulgence in an orgy of convenience. In any event, the motto "Eat, drink and be merry for tomorrow we die," is not conducive to saving, capital formation, or strong resistance to price increases.

The complexity of the causes of inflation suggests that there is a collective as well as a dispersed individual responsibility for the harm that results to both individuals and society. As yet, the authors have not seen an adequate theory for assigning either the collective or individual guilt.

BY WAY OF SUMMARY

In the practical order, business people must ask themselves if they have obtained their price as a result of free agreements that protect the legitimate interests of all, or if their profits result from power, fraud, ignorance, and passion. In many cases, they will have proportionate reasons for permitting or risking harm that they cannot prevent or mitigate at any reasonable cost. Finally, because they are an important part of society, they may have an obligation to work for the elimination of situations that provide excuses for giving less than perfect justice.

Competition is, of course, not an unmixed blessing. And because private power is potentially if not actually unjust, the establishment of prices that are both fair and socially acceptable will demand study and action beyond the direct control of business.

11

RELATIONS WITH COMPETITORS

INTRODUCTION

The ethics of business persons' relations with their competitors is not identical with the ethics of competition, which includes the study of the effect of acts on the competitive system itself. It is quite possible for an act to be fair and just to competitors and yet so injure the system that the government forbids the action by law. Unfortunately, our laws are not always clear as to whether competition, competitors, or the consuming public should have first place. Indeed, as we saw in the previous chapter, some laws protect the appearance of competition at the expense of the public. Moreover, there are increasing doubts as to the value of competition in many sectors of the economy. In the present chapter, we shall concentrate on relations with competitors rather than on the system itself. As a result, our conclusions always bear the qualification, explicit or implicit, *unless this is unethical because of its social effects.*

GENERAL PRINCIPLES

A competitor is ordinarily not an enemy but a rival. As a result, relations with competitors should be governed by basic ethics and the rules of fair play rather than by the ethics of self-defense and warfare. Unfortunately, an unethical competitor can turn rivalry into a ruthless battle. Therefore, there are cases where, *all legal remedies having been exhausted,* the ethics of self-defense comes into play. In the present chapter, we do not treat these cases, but assume that competitors are ethical and engaged in business rather than in jungle warfare.

As in every other sphere, it will be unethical to will a major harm to a competitor whether as a means or as an end. As in every game, however, not all can win. The ethical business person may often have a proportionate reason for permitting or risking harm to a competitor. Thus, if one wins away one's competitor's customers by offering truly superior service and low prices based on volume savings, one is hardly unethical. After all, the economy exists ultimately for the consumer and should reward those who do the best job, unless efficiency is unethical because of its social impact.

Because of the linkage between sellers and consumers, practically every practice that is unfair to consumers is also unfair to competitors, since it takes away business by means other than product, terms, and service. Fraudulent advertising, for example, not only bilks the buyer but robs a competitor of business to which he was entitled on the merits of the product. In the present chapter, we shall not reconsider all the cases taken up previously but concentrate to a large extent on those cases where the competitor is the primary victim.

DENIGRATION OF COMPETITORS

It is obviously wrong to lie about one's competitors or their products. The unfounded whispering campaign, which tells of insects found consistently in soft drinks, and the false rumor that a competitor's product contains harmful substances fall under this condemnation. It is not so easy to decide cases when the harm results from *truthful and founded* statements. The difficulty resides in the fact that even the truth, as we said in the chapter on secrecy, can sometimes cause more harm than good. The truth, indeed, can be a two-edged sword that cuts the user as well as the intended victim. Perhaps a competitor does use inferior materials, but the revelation of the fact may cast suspicion on the entire industry. To put it another way, the person who throws mud must be on guard lest some of it be blown back by the wind. On the other hand, silence can also be unethical if it exposes others to unnecessary harm. Each case must be carefully judged on its own merits. In general, the business person may and sometimes must make truthful though harmful statements about competitors in the following circumstances:

1. To prevent a competitor from cheating or harming a consumer.
2. To stop a competitor from using unfair practices. For example, one may warn a consumer that the competitor's product has not held up well in use, or one may point out that the competitor is engaging in deceptive advertising.

Despite these expectations, the good of the business community generally demands that truthful, if disparaging, statements be made in private or if possible to trade associations or law enforcement groups who have a legitimate concern. In particular, disparaging advertising should generally be avoided since its public nature may tend to lower confidence in an entire industry and not merely in the competitor. It is for this reason that most advertising groups are against comparative advertising.

A distinction should be made between disparagement by direct statements and disparagement by implication, since nearly every positive statement about the worth of one's own product implies in some way that the competing products are not as good. If it is a fact that product X is the best or the most economical, others must in some way be inferior. The implication is such an accepted part of American advertising that no one bothers about it, although such comparisons are forbidden by the laws of other nations. When the comparison is effectively meaningless, there is certainly no great ethical problem. In other cases, the implication may be harmful, or false, or both. An advertisement that puts all of its stress on the safety of electrical heating might imply that other forms are unsafe. If the statement is true, the ethics of the implication are to be judged by the rule given above. It would seem to us, however, that it would require less reason to permit harm from the implication of the truth than from a directly disparaging truthful statement. The reason is simple. If one were required to avoid all damaging implications, it would soon be impossible to say anything significant.

UNFAIR INTERFERENCE AND RELATED PRACTICES

It is possible to harm a competitor by interfering with his production and distribution. Thus, at one time, unethical competitors helped foment labor disputes and work stoppages as well as boycotts of a competitor's products. Such crude and clearly immoral practices are not too common today, but there are still cases involving the hiring away of key employees or the use of market power to move the competitor's products into a corner, if not off the shelf, in retail establishments. Our problem is to draw the line between unfair interference and legitimate competitive practices. Indeed, as a rule, the problem is not, in the fact of the interference, but in the method used to produce it. The key question is generally whether or not the interference results from providing more efficient service or from the intention to harm the competitor.

Hiring a competitor's workers as a means of harassment and of crippling his or her operation is unethical. Hiring the competitor's workers as a means of enlarging and improving one's own operation is both good business and good ethics. The ultimate effects on the competitor may be the same, but the intention, plus the potential benefits to consumers, make the difference. We assume, of course, that there was no breach of contract or of fiduciary relationships.

Employees should beware of job offers that contain conditions relating to the revelation of trade secrets. Not only is there the danger of cooperation in theft but also of personal loss. Experience shows that those who are dishonest in one area are dishonest in others. As noted in Chapter Seven, it is not always easy to draw the line between trade secrets and other information gained in the course of employment. However, integrity demands that an honest effort be made to distinguish cases and assure fairness to all.

In competing for shelf space in retail establishments, a salesperson is generally ethical so long as he or she gets favored spots on the basis of his product or of legitimate service to the storekeeper. Better design, packaging, displays, price, advertising supports, and delivery are all part of the service. Unfair competition enters with extortion, bribery, kickbacks, and the granting of discriminatory advertising allowances or brokerage fees. In these areas, the Robinson-Patman Act should be consulted, since many of these practices are covered by law as well as by ethics.[1] Those who want to complete the catalogue of unethical acts in this area should refer back to Chapter Ten and look ahead to our treatment of relations with dealers in Chapter Twelve.

A few practices are difficult to analyze, since the harm to a competitor is offset by benefits to the consumer. Merchants, for example, are indignant when a competitor advertises a price reduction on a specific nationally advertised product that is "fair traded." Such a practice hurts but may also help consumers to get information about real bargains. The advertising may be unethical if it breaks a real contract or violates a just law, but it cannot be condemned merely because it hurts a competitor. This brings us to the difficult question of price cutting.

PRICE CUTTING

Price competition is supposed to be the heart of the market economy. Yet, price cutting is a dirty word because so many people fear price competition and dream of price stability. Thus, we may have schizophrenia, if not hypocricy, when business praises competition while trying to avoid it in the area of prices. Moreover, it is an attitude that complicates ethical analysis by substituting slogans and epithets for thinking.

Like most questions in the present chapter, the ethics of price cutting is a question of intention, and of means, and not merely of effects on a given competitor. Indeed, price cuts are, in general, a legitimate and desirable competitive tool whose harmful side effects on competitors are offset by the benefits to consumers and to the economy as a whole. In the ideal world of the perfect market, price cutting would be the most ethical way of competing. The reason is that in such a never-never world, no one seller could really hurt anyone. In the real world, however, price cuts backed by power can be used as a club to obtain advantages that have nothing to do with quality or service to the consumer.

In the concrete, we condemn price cutting that is *intended* to harm a com-

[1]Wright Patman, *Complete Guide to the Robinson-Patman Act* (Englewood Cliffs, New Jersey: Prentice-Hall, 1963), pp. 102–147.

petitor. This is particularly reprehensible when the ultimate aim is the establishment of a power that can be used to exploit customers. A test for the presence of such unethical intentions is found in the question: "Is this price cut calculated to help the business without exploiting consumers either now or in the future?"

Undercost selling is often, but not necessarily, a sign of the unethical intention mentioned above. A company may ethically sell under cost to liquidate inventory that is tying up capital. It may ethically use "loss leaders" as a promotion so long as its general price level covers expenses. Often it may be necessary and ethical to sell below cost in an effort to recoup at least some fixed costs in hard times. All of these price cuts may hurt competitors, but they are ethical, since they are not purposely aimed at either harming competitors or at exploiting present or future buyers.

The ethics in this area are complicated by the existence of state laws on sales below cost. Since these often forbid sales below cost because they might tend to create a monopoly or divert trade or even lessen competition, they cover more actions than our principles in the present chapter. The exceptions allowed in these laws are also allowed in ethics, so that they can provide a catalogue of proportionate reasons. The following are typical exceptions: a bona fide clearance sale advertised as such; sales of perishable merchandise to forestall loss; imperfect or damaged merchandise sold as such; discontinued merchandise sold as such; a final liquidation; sales for charitable purposes and to relief agencies; sales to government; sales made in good faith to meet competition; sales by court order; sales to employees of tools and the like used in the trade. Not all exceptions hold in all states, nor do all exceptions in ethics apply in law. As a result, it is necessary to know the local regulations.

What has just been said can be applied to almost all industries characterized by an approximation to real competition. The careful student of ethics, however, will see that there are situations where additional factors must be considered. The following cases will indicate some of the problems that the ethical business person must face in this area.

1. A building contractor, in bad financial condition, makes a very low bid on a job in order to recoup some of his fixed costs, keep his staff, and stay in business for a while longer. When the demand for buildings is low and the number of builders high, such a situation may become common. This can be disastrous for the industry. In the first place, such bidding may make buyers unwilling to pay prices that allow a reasonable profit. In the second place, it may tempt builders to conspire to rig bids in order to protect themselves. In the third place, the desperate builder may go bankrupt in the course of fulfilling his contract and leave the job unfinished. Finally, there is a temptation to cut corners, substitute lower grade materials, and otherwise violate the contract in order to break even.

The desperate bidder we have described may intend to fulfill the contract according to specifications and so have a completely ethical intention. Does he, however, have a proportionate reason for running all the risks we have described? In most cases, the bidder has not caused the situation. Often too, his failure to bid low will not remedy the situation. His bid may be below cost or close to it, but it is a reasonable means of cutting loss and staying in business. By every ordinary criterion, he seems to have a proportionate reason for making his offer; yet risks remain.

Actually, we are dealing with one of those situations where competition, as a fairly orderly process, has broken down. The obvious solutions, moreover, are either forbidden by law or repugnant to many business people. The problem could be solved by the industry's setting up standards and qualifications, but this would look like a conspiracy in restraint of trade. Indeed, it could very easily become just that. The second solution would involve the use of law to enforce strict bonding requirements or to forbid bids below cost. Such a law, of course, would create problems about entry into the business and involve more supervision than many would like.

This type of problem illustrates the need for broad industry and social cooperation, which considers the impact of both business and legislation on many groups. The fact that isolated individuals are relatively powerless to prevent the evil creates an obligation to work for such broad control as will minimize the harmful effects.

2. The owner of a small but efficient firm with unused capacity wants to lower prices in order to increase volume and profits. He has, of course, every right to do so. Indeed, it is in the interest of the public. He fears, however, that larger though less efficient firms will retaliate by cutting prices even below cost and so nullify his attempt to improve his business.

The producer in question is certainly justified in not cutting prices in such a situation. His larger competitors have not made any actual threat, in which case they would be guilty of extortion, but the effects are such that these harmful results follow. A competitor is robbed of legitimate freedom; and the public is deprived of the benefits of price cuts. On the face of it we have a real evil without anyone committing a clearly unethical act. This is a result of the fact that real power works even when it is not used. It deters even if its possessor does not actually threaten to use it. Once again we are faced with a problem of competition that cannot be solved by the individual conscience but requires broad social cooperation and legislation.

3. A large and efficient company could make a greater profit with lowered prices and increased volume. The owner is in no danger of retaliation and, indeed, will probably drive his smaller and less efficient competitors out of business. Such a course of action, however, would attract the attention of the anti-trust watchdogs and possibly lead to annoying suits. As a result, he administers prices and protects his less efficient competitors. In the end, the public pays more for products than it should or would in a truly competitive

economy. Once again no one has performed a clearly unethical act, but the evil results. Once again, the solution can only be found by changing the laws and extending our understanding of the good in true competition. All too often we have maintained the appearance of competition while suffering from the evils of monopoly. Until such changes are made, it is difficult to accuse the business person who does not compete on price of committing an unethical act.

These cases should indicate that the ethical problems concerning the relationships of competitors cannot be considered aside from the relationship to consumers. In addition, they should show the necessity of supplementing individual ethical decisions by legal measures designed to assure that there is sufficient social cooperation to prevent or mitigate harmful effects that cannot be controlled by individuals.

COOPERATION AMONG COMPETITORS

Although our anti-trust law forbids cooperation that is detrimental to consumers or the economy as a whole, there are large areas in business where cooperation is in the best interests of all parties in the economic process. To a certain extent, trade associations are expressions of the need for cooperation. Unfortunately, many trade associations are purely defensive organizations and do not exhibit a creative approach to common problems. Despite this, the general obligation to operate one's business efficiently in the service of the consumer would seem to demand that business people look to greater cooperation within the existing legal framework. There are even some areas where they should work to change the framework so that they may better serve the public. The airlines, which cooperate by sharing information on maintenance, safety, and passenger handling, have each found profits from this procedure. Similarly, many small grocers have found that their very survival depends on cooperative buying and advertising. There are many other areas where cooperation may be the clue to future progress. We may ask the following questions: Is secrecy necessary in all research projects? Could cooperation here limit waste? Would not cooperative limitation of advertising for products with a stable global demand increase everyone's profits? Are there not areas in which standardized terminology and packaging could reduce shipping and marketing costs without crippling imagination and initiative?

Some firms are coming to realize that cooperation by licensing patents may also be beneficial at the same time that it helps the public. It is even possible that a wide sharing of all sorts of information would actually increase everyone's profits without harming the public. Here and now, we do not wish to take a definite stand on any of these questions. It is suggested, however, that there may be real positive obligations in this area—obligations that arise from concern for the good of the company as well as for the legitimate interests of consumers.

UNETHICAL COOPERATION AND COMPETITION

Illegal and/or unethical cooperation, whether it be conspiracy or an informal imitative venture, exists when competitors combine, not in the interests of real productive and distributive efficiency, but in order to exploit the weakness of buyers by power and fraud. While the main point has been developed sufficiently in the previous chapter, some of the underlying causes of such unethical cooperation are pertinent to a consideration of relations with competitors.

Sellers do not really like the true competitive process that will discipline them if they fail or slacken their efforts. This is particularly true if there is a buyer's market or sporadic demand. In addition, if the seller has high fixed costs, real price competition can easily turn profits into losses. As a result, such sellers want to insulate themselves from price competition and uncertainty. When this is done by deceiving buyers or cooperating against them, we have unethical conduct.

While the means used to insulate oneself from competition are unethical in many cases, we must face the fact that in some cases the business person is trying to avoid some evils that can harm not only the company but the industry and even the public. We may then condemn the means and still sympathize with some of the goals of these business people.

Competition that leads to monopoly may rob the public of even the limited benefits of oligopoly. Thus, real monopoly will demand government control of prices and frequently stop the benefits of such non-price competition as innovation, quality control, and better service. Whether the benefits of one system outweigh the benefits of another is a moot question. It is certain, however, that sellers do not have a right to make a unilateral decision and then enforce it by unethical means. Some are interested in price, and they should be able to negotiate a free purchase untrammeled by fraud or coercion. It may be that many industries should be monopolies controlled in the public interest. This decision, however, can only be made by the society as a whole and not by private individuals.

Competition that leads to chaotic price changes certainly does not benefit a company, an industry, or most buyers. However, the decision as to whether or not the value of stability outweighs the values of competition should not be made unilaterally and enforced unethically. Sound values and the ideals of our economy demand that both buyer and seller participate in negotiating truly free contracts of sale and purchase.

THE MORAL ATMOSPHERE OF COMPETITION

The ethics of competition cannot be divorced from the ethics of relations with workers, suppliers, stockholders, customers, and society as a whole. For this reason, nearly every chapter in this book has something to do with the ethical problems arising from relations with competitors. It must be repeated, therefore, that the attitude towards competition and business itself will be a controlling factor in the application of the principles developed to cover all of these areas.

If competition is viewed as a form of warfare in which the object is not to serve the consumer but to destroy the competitor, we can expect a steady disintegration of standards. In war, after all, no weapon has been banned until obsolete, and every practice has been justified in some way on the grounds of survival. While competition is not, by nature, warfare but rather a race to serve the public, there are cases where an unfair competitor turns the game into a battle. Where the law offers no remedy, the temptation is strong to retaliate in kind and to meet force and trickery with force and trickery.

The truly ethical business people must resist the temptation lest they find that they have won the battle and lost the war. Unethical retaliation for unethical attack destroys confidence in business and introduces chaos where order should reign. It substitutes tricks for real competence and leads to a weakening of all human ideals. The correct solution is not unethical retaliation but an effort to unite the industry behind true ideals and to secure such legal regulation as is necessary to protect the honest merchant. Only in this way can people protect their souls as well as their businesses.

When conspiracy, theft, and bribery become the pattern in an industry, costs are forced up and honesty, even within companies, is diminished. The increased costs often lead to a decrease in quality and services with the result that business is less efficient in serving the public. We know of one country where advertisers blackmailed their advertising agencies into kickbacks until the agencies ended up doing little more than passing on orders for space in newspapers. When this situation became widespread, the development of advertising techniques and services was paralyzed with the result that the distribution system, already poor, stagnated.

It should be recalled that a competitor's tactics are not unethical merely because they pinch. To prove unethical conduct, one must show either that the intention is evil or that the competitor is permitting harm with no proportionate reason. Perhaps average human beings cannot make such distinctions when they feel that they are the victim. However, unless such distinctions and allowances are made, competition can degenerate into total war.

For all of these reasons, business must recognize that it often needs an outside referee and that government can be the friend of the honest business person even though there is a price to pay.

BY WAY OF SUMMARY

In general, it is unethical to will major harm to a competitor. At the same time if one competitor suffers because others are truly more efficient and more responsive to customers, this is not unethical since it results from true service to the economic life of the society. It should be noted, however, that what is unfair to consumers is with rare exceptions also unfair to competitors.

Although cooperation between competitors is generally both illegal and unethical since it tends to exploit consumers, there are cases where cooperation can benefit all actors in the economic order. On the other hand, when competition degenerates into warfare, self-defense rather than fairness tends to determine what is minimally ethical.

12

STOCKHOLDERS, DEALERS, AND SUPPLIERS

INTRODUCTION

In the good old days, when businesses were managed by their owners, and firms did not tower over their suppliers and dealers, the world of business ethics was considerably simpler. In those days one could look out for one's own interests within the limits set by the fairly clear rights of others. Even in the days of industrial capitalism, when the manager worked for a tightly held corporation or family business, one still knew to whom one was responsible and for what. Today, however, we live in a world of collective capitalism where managers are the employees of a corporation whose legal owners are so numerous as to form a faceless mob, and so powerless as individuals that they often have little control over what is technically their own property. In addition to this, the manager of the giant collective enterprise has power over the lives and destiny not only of the workers but over less powerful firms, which may depend on his or her company in a special way. The existence of this power over suppliers and dealers, plus a changing relationship to stockholders, creates special ethical problems for the manager of the large corporation. The problems are all the more difficult, since we are not always sure of what the relationship is or what significance it has for others.

In an earlier chapter, we solved several ethical problems by considering the manager as the agent of the corporation and of its stockholders. Although managers are certainly this, they are a great deal more in many cases. Such professionals are, at least in the case of the large corporations, the mediators of the overlapping if not conflicting interests of investors, workers, dealers, suppliers, the local community, and the national economy. Managers are at once executives, legislators, and supreme court justices while not elected by those whose interests they must reconcile. Often they have not even been chosen in any significant sense by the stockholders. Within limits, they are frequently not accountable to anyone but peers in the managerial aristocracy. Like other human beings, managers of such corporations must anticipate reactions to their decisions and fear retaliation by other economic agents, if not by the government, but they have more freedom and often more power than elected representatives in the government. More often than not, managers have little fear of being put out of their jobs once they have reached the top. The top executives may not always appreciate their freedom and power, for they are acutely aware of the union, competitors, and the government. If such executives have any sensitivity, they are also aware of the obstacles that exist within their own organizations. For all of this, managers enjoy considerable freedom and power without, in most cases, having any formal constitution to guide them in the use of it. Perhaps it would be most accurate to say that managers have wide discretionary powers for which they are ordinarily answerable largely to themselves or to a few peers.

The situation we are describing is neither an accident nor the result of deliberate comprehensive planning. It evolved as business persons and society made a series of adjustments to constantly changing needs. For a long time, most people were not even aware of the cumulative effect of the changes so that they still spoke in terms of an ethic that no longer covered all the duties and responsibilities of management. Now, however, increasing attention is being given to the actual state of affairs and to the development of norms of behavior that will apply to the new world of business. In the process of adapting and changing, the norms may not always be satisfactory. Yet, as has been noted several times before, the attempt to isolate problems and develop principles is a vital necessity.

RELATIONS WITH STOCKHOLDERS

Although stockholders are legally the owners of the company, their legal claims against it are minimal. There are some legal remedies, but the stockholder's ability to use them is sometimes limited by ignorance and by the cost of initiating and sustaining a suit against a group with vast resources. Actually, most stockholders do not appear interested in exerting any control over their company so long as it is profitable either in terms of dividends or the increasing value of its stock. This is reflected in the attitude of management, which often sees its first loyalty to the company itself rather than to the stockholders. The manager realizes that the stockholder must be served in some way, but this is not necessarily the chief concern. This is as it should be, for other claimants on the corporation have more urgent needs and make greater contributions to the corporation. This fact needs to be stressed lest the ethics of the manager be unduly narrowed. As Berle has pointed out,[1] the stockholder does not, as a rule, invest in the corporation but in the stock quotation. In the case of new stocks and bonds, the buyer is a real investor in the sense that he or she adds to the store of capital, but ordinary stock purchases do not allocate capital so much as they redistribute liquid claims. Thus, in the vast majority of cases, the stockholder does not supply capital and often does not take much risk. Indeed, if it were not for legal limitations, the more prosperous companies could buy up all of their own stock and finance most of their operations and expansions out of retained earnings, bond issues, or loans from banks. In such a case, the corporation would own itself, and we would no longer have the fiction of private ownership.[2]

All of this does not mean that the stockholder has no rights but that they are not as clear and simple as some would lead us to believe. Furthermore, even though it may not allocate capital very often, the stock market is necessary for the performance of other socially useful functions. As a result, management may have obligations to potential stockholders and to society as a whole even when it does not have direct duties regarding actual stockholders.

Berle believes that stock and other forms of passive property serve the following functions.[3] They can form a reserve of liquid property to provide for old age and to free people for self-realization. They can help to support a leisure class, which can devote itself to important social tasks that do not have a large monetary reward. Furthermore, they provide resources for non-commercial institutional activities of foundations, universities, and the like. Finally, the institution of passive property makes it possible to tax inheritances, gifts, and capital gains.

REPORTING

Stocks and bonds can fulfill these important functions efficiently only if those who buy and sell them have adequate information about the position of various firms in the economy. Since management is the only group that can supply this information, we believe it has an obligation to do so. It is a social obligation to potential stockholders and not merely a duty towards those who actually possess stock at the present time. How much information should be given is a debatable question, but as information becomes more and more crucial, there will probably be an increased demand for it.

In theory, the certified annual report of a corporation and its K9 report to the SEC, take care of the necessary reporting. Unfortunately, accepted ac-

[1]Adolph A. Berle, *The American Economic Republic* (New York: Harcourt, Brace & World, 1963), pp. 129 ff.

[2]See this worked out by Andrew Hacker in his introduction to *The Corporation Take-Over* (New York: Harper & Row, 1964), pp. 3–6.

[3]Berle, *op. cit.*, pp. 47–51.

counting principles allow so much leeway that the information may not be adequate. It is possible that three companies with identical income and identical expenses could report three widely different profit figures, depending on the method used to record certain expenditures. Some tobacco companies report taxes on sales as a part of sales, with the result that sales are inflated while earnings as a percentage appear to be low. Income level accounting is still not too common in reports to outsiders, though obviously management must use it for its own purposes. Often, when many assets are intangible or tied up in research that represents a potential asset, there is no way of knowing the true value of the company. Furthermore, from a broader social point of view, the annual report gives no information about the social costs of the business, so that it is difficult to tell whether the company really earned a profit or merely enjoyed some privilege and exploited some advantage to which it had no right. Even when there has not been exploitation of this sort, the business ethics of the future will certainly demand a social audit and the reporting of this to both stockholders and the public. That, however, is not the present reality.

Serious students of accounting and social problems are very interested in these problems of reporting, but the public, even the educated public, is so ignorant of what is at stake that progress in this area is slow. Yet the need for more and better information is growing, and with it, the obligation to provide it. Management's concrete obligations, however, may be difficult to define. Furthermore, in the absence of uniformity or legal regulation beyond those already in force, unilateral decisions may only add more confusion. Once again we are at a point where we need broader social cooperation.

Although we cannot solve the problem completely, it should be obvious that reporting must be truthful and reasonably complete within the present system. The public has a right to know the accounting methods used and any significant definition of costs and capitalization. To put it another way, information should not only be adequate but phrased in such a way that the ordinary stockholder can follow the report and make some intelligent judgment.

While the public accountants may develop new terminology and methods of presenting information, they cannot serve the public without management's cooperation. So long as management uses and follows accepted accounting procedures, the Certified Public Accountant must approve the presentation even though he or she does not agree with it completely. The norm for both groups—accountants and managers—should not be accepted principles, but rather, adequate reporting judged according to the needs of the stockholding public.

Pressure from the Securities and Exchange Commission (SEC), the Federal Trade Commission (FTC), the Stock exchanges, and the various accounting boards has done much to improve reporting. The debate does continue over reporting by product line and division which would reveal what is hidden in the consolidated reports.

It would appear, however, that there is room for considerable improvement if management is to be publicly accountable and of service to the economy as a whole. Moreover, as we intimated in our chapter on secrecy, it may be that public accountability will even involve the revelation of information that has traditionally been considered the property or prerogative of only the innermost councils of business.

Realistically, reporting and revelation of data will not solve all problems. In the economic order, there are no such simple solutions. However, it must be admitted that both as a check and as a reminder of management's broader functions, better reporting has its role to play in moving the American Economy towards a more efficient and more just operation.

MANAGERIAL COMPENSATION

The increasing need for information and adequate reporting will serve to illustrate one of the new problems that has developed. The older problems can be illustrated in a few words about executive compensation, dividends, and the use of retained earnings.

Whether managers are considered to have their primary obligation to the company or to the stockholder, the firm's income is not theirs to do with as they will. At the same time the actual relationships between managers and directors and their relative freedom from stockholder's control can give managers broad powers which can be abused.

What are we to say of the ethics of a company that continues to pay handsome salaries to executives although operations have stopped almost completely? What principles should govern the granting of stock options, which may dilute the shareholder's equity? What is to be said of generous pensions, which have not been voted in advance but are invented at the moment of retirement?

It is difficult to give precise norms for these situations. All sorts of compensations may be justified if necessary to attract and hold highly skilled executives who are in short supply. So too, industry levels may give some rough indication of what is reasonable compensation. This still leaves us with the question of whether it is unethical to pay more than necessary or more than industry levels. Actually, fairness can probably only be established by a free agreement among those whose interests are involved. This job can be done by a truly independent board of directors. It might even be done by getting stockholders to approve a formula which provides guidelines. At the very least, fairness would be increased if stockholders were given full details not only about the compensation but about its potential impact on earnings and the value of the stock. No matter what method is used, there should be an actual rather than theoretical accountability for decisions that affect stockholders. Once again we must face the fact that ethics can be as much a question of designing adequate institutions as of formulating abstract principles.

DIVIDENDS AND RETAINED EARNINGS

Managers' decisions about the distribution of earnings have ethical implications, for they are handling other people's money no matter what the nature of their legal rights. Perhaps there would be no problem if managers were true "economists" endowed with lofty rationality. Unfortunately, managers are human beings with mixed motives, some of which may be at odds with sound business practices. There are managers who expand their companies not because they will be more profitable or more stable but because it flatters their ego to do so. This is not unlike the case of the executive who invests heavily in advertising and public relations to make himself look good rather than because it is necessary for the company. Those who doubt the existence of such people should talk to the public relations expert who is given the job of making a five-foot executive look six feet tall. In addition, the personalities and irrational fears of managers will often lead them to make decisions which are safe rather than profitable. Some of the famous raiding expeditions have come about when conservative managements have created a temptation by understanding assets or by piling up large cash reserves.

There is also a temptation to view retained earnings as a source of capital that entails little obligation. However, this may not be in the interest of the stockholders if they could invest their dividends more profitably elsewhere in the market. Executives, of course, tend to overestimate the profitability of reinvestment in their own firm. This, unfortunately, not only deprives the stockholders of making their own choice but means that resources in the economy as a whole are not allocated effectively even on the basis of supply and demand.

Once again precise norms cannot be easily formulated. A reasonably clear-cut dividend policy would clarify the situation with regard to retained earnings and dividends.

Much the same can be said about management decisions as to financial and asset structures. Conservatism in this area can be produced either by fear or greed. A small debt may cut down fear of failure, but it can also increase the cost of capital. So too, cash resulting from depreciation, but not used to buy new capital assets, can stagnate the firm. In short, nearly every aspect of the management of a firm's finances involves control not only of money but of fears and ambitions, when these run counter to the manager's obligations to be efficient.

These last remarks illustrate a point familiar to business psychologists but often overlooked especially by young persons in middle management. The character and values of top managers are almost as important to the efficient operation of the firm and the economy as are their knowledge and skills. Good ethics can help to build character and implement values so that ultimately they may be responsible for a major contribution to society in spite of the fact that the opportunist and the narrow-minded individual may see them as obstacles.

STOCKHOLDER RESPONSIBILITY

While corporate managers have serious ethical obligations, so do stockholders. The moral responsibilities of stockholders must, however, be discussed in direct relationship to their rights and actual power. It can be argued that the degree of responsibility to be placed on the stockholders to respond to what appear to be immoral practices by their corporation is then directly proportionate to their ability and power to do so.

Because power or ability to effect change is, in large measure, relative to rights, a brief discussion of stockholder rights is in order. Holders of common stock have traditionally had the following rights: they have a right to vote for the directors of the corporation and a right to vote for the CPA firm that will audit the books. However, because the nominations of directors and the CPA firms are pretty well controlled by the present officers, such a right to vote is often without great consequence. Shareholders of common stock have a right to a dividend "if the directors declare one." Shareholders of common stock also have a right to a pro rata share of the liquidated company, after everyone else has been paid off. Finally, common stockholders have a right, under certain conditions, to put policy items on the agenda of the annual stockholder's meeting and, as always, to vote their shares in response to the items up for consideration on the agenda.

As is perhaps clear by now, stockholders have few significant rights and so relatively little power or effect on the policies of the corporation. This position becomes more persuasive once the distinction is made between large and small stockholders, a distinction in practice tantamount to one made between significant and generally insignificant shareholders. The large stockholders are most often, for example, pension funds, mutual funds, insurance companies, foundations, and charitable institutions. These shareholders tend to vote with management most of the time, if they vote their shares at all. In the case of an extraordinary or very serious conflict of interests between such a major stockholder and the corporation, this sort of shareholder will just divest itself of its stock and invest elsewhere. The point here is that unless mass selling of stock by common stockholders occurs, and this would include these major or large stockholders, the effect of a stockholder protest aimed at substantially altering company policy or halting a designated corporate investment or venture will be insignificant.

In light of the fact that stockholder rights, limited as they are, tend to limit stockholder power and capacity to effect change, it might be argued that holders of common stock have no significant obligations to monitor or attempt to affect corporate investments of questionable moral character. This, however, is not necessarily the case.

While it could be argued that the responsibility of the stockholders to address and protest questionable practices of their corporation must in general be gauged in proportion to their power and capacity to effect change, their responsibility need not be solely gauged in this manner. In our judgment, stockholders might have obligations to protest such practices even if they cannot effect immediate change. This position gains strength once it is realized that the effects of stockholder protest are not limited to changing this or that investment policy or to specifically redirecting the path of the corporation at a given time.

In the absence of such immediate effects, shareholders still have a moral obligation to protest unfair practices being engaged in by their corporations. Such protest and commentary, which must be made explicit to the company and, in particularly egregious circumstances (such as the Nestle infant formula scandal), to society as a whole, will serve to set a tone for future business practice. Even if the corporation did not suffer a serious financial or public relations defeat at the time of a strong stockholder protest, such fundamentally democratic action and public commentary on the part of shareholders will, in the long-run, help create a more moral climate in light of which society, as a whole, will come to examine corporate activities. In this regard, stockholders must take greater interest in the activities of the corporations in which they invest. They are thus obligated to look beyond whether their company is generating a profit for them. Shareholders aware of a serious social injustice, either present or foreseen, must expose that injustice as a matter of moral obligation and good citizenship—including world citizenship.

RELATIONS WITH DEALERS

Like the stockholders, dealers are generally not members of the firm. They are, however, more closely related to it than an ordinary buyer, so that the long-enduring relationship of buyer and seller has special characteristics. Furthermore, dealers are, to a large extent, part of the manufacturer's face to the public. It is for this reason that dealerships are so common in areas of business where a product may need a great deal of service or involve some difficult installation. Dealers on their own side, being as a rule less powerful than their suppliers, are dependent for their continued existence on the suppliers and their forebearance in the use of power. The ethical problems in this area arise, not only from the relationship between buyer and seller, but from the relationship of both to the consuming public. As noted in previous chapters, the two must not enter into a conspiracy against the ultimate purchaser who has a right to a fair contract of sale.

Producers have a variety of power tools that they can use in disciplining dealers. Most of these tactics are legal, but they can be unethical if used to enforce provisions or extort concessions that were not a part of the original free contract. The producer can, for example, withdraw advertising funds or financing, though this will be legal only if withdrawn from all dealers. In other cases, the manufacturer can delay shipments or fail to follow the dealers' preference. Such tactics can be extremely damaging at peak seasons when prompt delivery of reorders is the key to profits.

Dealers, of course, can provoke such retaliation by not living up to their contracts. Dealers have been known to tamper with mileage on cars so that the manufacturer's service representative does not know when a warrantee has expired. Car dealers have also been known to charge the factory for warranteed service that was not given. Some push hot items through second-hand lots and hurt other dealers.

While a manufacturer may rightly object to many of these practices, the remedy is in the courts or in refusal to renew the franchise, rather than in a kind of private penal system. Sometimes, indeed, there is need for readjustment of conditions which tempt the dealer. For example, if the factory flat-rate manual for car repairs underestimates the cost of the job, the dealer will be tempted to report a higher cost repair in order to break even. So too, if the manufacturer's terms prevent a dealer from competing locally, the dealer will try to save him or herself no matter what the contract says.

The old-fashioned tie-in contract, which forced the dealers to carry a full line whether they wanted to or not, is a prime example of the unjust use of power against dealers. Although such practices are theoretically illegal, in some cases the practice continues. For example, in order to obtain the brands they want liquor store owners may be forced to take inferior merchandise which is difficult to move. Such practices are forms of extortion. They also have undesirable effects on the market insofar as they can insulate the manufacturers or processors from the effects of demand even as the dealers are forced to assume unnecessary inventory costs.

A similar evil results from full-line forcing, where the producer is able to refuse to sell anything unless the dealer agrees not to trade with competitors. While the evil of this is clear, it should be distinguished from the exclusive agency by which a given retailer has the exclusive rights to handle the product in his or her territory. In this case, the retailer is generally more than glad to accept the contract which does not force competition out of the territory. This is a good exchange as the manufacturer grants a valuable right in an exclusive territory, and the retailer has a real trade advantage.

At the present time there is some doubt as to the social utility of franchises, since they can be used to reduce competition. Thus the automobile manufacturers object to their dealers' selling to discounters who will force down the prices of the cars. Such control is able to cut down the savings resulting from volume purchasing and reduce the freedom to buy a car without purchasing the dealer's unwanted services. While this issue cannot be settled in a few words, the reader should be aware that the cooperation of manufacturer and dealer can considerably reduce consumers' freedom and force them to buy a joint product at a higher price.

Fair trade prices, as previously noted, are another example of where the agreement between the manufacturer and dealer limits the freedom of the consumer by reducing the impact of competition. As is often the case, however, the steady pressure of the public, which wants to purchase the product without the services, will destroy the agreement unless the courts use their power to protect the so-called Fair trade contract.

A great many ethical problems can arise when either the dealer or manufacturer violates the terms of sale. Manufacturers who grant an exclusive territory and then sell within that territory from the home office are acting unethically. Similarly, the dealer benefiting from a cooperative advertising budget offends if he or she pads the total bill so that the manufacturer pays more than the agreed share. This is, merely, to say that nearly everything we have said about the relationship of buyers and sellers in general, applies to the dealer as well.

SOLUTIONS

There will be fewer problems in this area if dealers combine to trade with the manufacturer. Indeed, where this has been done, or where an individual dealer is extremely powerful, the results have been more equitable. Unfortunately, the result is not always lower prices for consumers, who cannot organize their power with the same precision and impact.

Actually, the solution may be in the provision for some form of due process through which dealers can bring complaints at a reasonable cost. At least one of the automobile manufacturers has adopted such a policy with varying success. As in other areas where there are no clear-cut standards to cover many problems, due process reduces the chances of the arbitrary application and assures that judgments will not be completely unilateral.

RELATIONS WITH SUPPLIERS

The suppliers, like the stockholders and the dealers, are not members of the firm. At times, however, they may be so dependent on a particular customer or so inferior in power to the firm that special problems arise. In addition, problems arise when suppliers and manufacturers make agreements that are unfair either to competitors or to ultimate consumers. While previous chapters have covered many of these problems, a few particular problems will illustrate the types of situations that can arise.

A large department store chain is in a position to get substantial contributions to a special advertising budget by threatening to withdraw business. Such a practice is equivalent to the open or covert forcing of a supplier to assume a company's promotion costs. Similarly, a big buyer can sometimes force the financing of its operation by pushing the cost of credit back on to the supplier. We know of one case where a major American company was consistently three and four months behind in its payments to a small business whose cash position was only fair. The small operator was in no position to bargain or enforce reasonable payment schedules, so that it had to pay interest on money borrowed to meet payrolls and other current expenses.

Force, of course, can be used to obtain special prices, financing, and contributions, and to extort special treatment in scheduling and specifications that harm not only the supplier but the buyer's competitors. For example, the supplier can be forced to delay the production and delivery of long-standing orders to accommodate an immediate need of the big buyer. The more dependent the supplier is on a given customer, the more likely it is for such situations to occur. Indeed, in those cases where a supplier has only one real customer, the entire operation may depend on the good will of the buyer. Ethical firms, of course, seek to avoid such situations, since they create an ethical limitation on their freedom to shift business as they see fit.

Occasionally, buyers use potential suppliers against one another by quoting fictitious low bids that will tempt the hungry supplier into accepting contracts that give little profit. As noted in our discussion of contractors who bid below or very close to cost, this sort of deception can lead to the disruption of an industry and to the proliferation of cheating designed to recoup the losses of the supplier. Similar deception can take place when the buyer bills the supplier for costs supposedly incurred because of mistakes on the part of the buyer. Thus a steel erector is often in a position to backcharge a steel fabricator for supposed errors, when actually the charge is being used to lower the erector's true cost as provided for in the contract. Such practices are so unethical that they hardly need further comment.

The shoe can be on the other foot when the supplier is the larger and more powerful firm, but the fact of injustice is the same. These problems, however, have been adequately treated in the chapter on the relations with buyers and in our section on the relationship with dealers.

Obviously every unfair advantage in this area harms the competitors of the favored party. The courts, for example, are suspicious of situations where a manufacturer sells to a company while buying from one of the customer's subsidiaries. Such a relationship may give the manufacturer the power to extort or simply attract reciprocal purchases from suppliers. Whether the situation involves companies in related or unrelated industries, such reciprocity can give an unfair advantage to one party.

Suppliers and buyers, like other agents in the economic process, should not enter into conspiracy against the interests of third parties, such as the ultimate consumer. Buyers who agree to any price because they can easily pass on the increased costs to their customers are acting unfairly, since they have an obligation to be as efficient as possible within the limits of fairness. Furthermore, when high prices are agreed upon carelessly and with the knowledge that less efficient competitors cannot pay them, there is another example of anti-competitive practices. Often there is no legal remedy for such actions, but the unethical intentions and the harmful effects are there, nevertheless.

BY WAY OF SUMMARY

The present chapter not only raises a series of questions and illustrates the variety of problems that can occur, but points up the need for looking at actual relationships rather than at theoretical ones. Indeed, a thorough study of these areas would unearth bewildering complexities. Do the various classes of shareholders have different rights from an ethical as well as from a legal point of view? What are the obligations of management in the truly speculative ventures where stock represents real risk capital? Do we, as Eells suggested over two decades ago, need a real corporate constitution which governs its relations with all the various classes of satellites such as suppliers and dealers?[4] What problems are posed by holding companies and their control, but not complete ownership, of subsidiaries?

There are enough problems here to keep both amateurs and professionals busy for many years. These, however, are simple problems compared to those which arise because of the relationship of business to such non-economic groups as the union, the local community, and the world as a whole.

[4]Richard Eells, *The Government of Corporations* (New York: Free Press, 1962), pp. 82–88.

13
RELATIONS WITH UNIONS, LOCAL COMMUNITIES, AND THE ENVIRONMENT

INTRODUCTION

Earlier in the text we considered the relationship of the firm to groups and individuals whose interests were primarily economic. Now we must consider the relationship between business and typically nonbusiness groups, including the environment. While unions and various local communities have strong economic interests, they are not exclusively economic societies. The environment, of course, has no economic "interests" at all. However, all three of these fundamentally noneconomic or nonbusiness entities affect and are affected by the business community.

In this chapter, we will attempt to point up some of the problems inherent in situations where the interests of unions and local communities come into conflict with each other as well as with the interests of the business community. Given the enormous potential for conflict among these groups, it must be noted that there is often a strong temptation to use power, whether economic or political, to win the upper hand.

In many ways, it was because of the economic power of business during the great growth period of the American economy that business was able to disregard (granted sometimes justifiably), the social costs of its operations. When water, timber, minerals, and air were assumed to be unlimited in supply, and the need for products was perceived to be limited in scope, getting the job done took first place. Today, however, as the world shrinks and the population expands, the hidden costs of business have become more obvious and the public less willing to bear them. The pollution of our streams, the poisoning of the air, and the scarring of the landscape are all costs often transferred from business to the general public.

It is clear that business had not always thought to internalize what it understood to be external costs of production. However, there is little debate today about the fact that businesses should take up responsibility for addressing environmental problems in proportion to their causal role relative to these problems. Yet, as we shall see, there is a strong argument for business to assume a less reactionary and more affirmative attitude in the future regarding ecological concerns.

THE UNION

Although unions can be described in economic terms and be considered as similar to a firm which controls the supply and cost of labor, it is more complex than this. Unions have social and political dimensions. They are concerned not only with wages, but with working conditions and with the distribution of power in the economy. They can, on occasion, be a major political force, although in the United States they have tended to play down this role. The unique nature of the unions is recognized and protected in law, and although technically private associations, they are so related to the public interest that there is an increasing demand for public accountability. On the whole, however, unions still enjoy great freedom and privilege; the law assumes that they are the underdogs and seeks to equalize the power of labor and management in the hope that greater fairness will result from collective bargaining. The unions, however, are not always the weaker parties. Small business people feel threatened by the big unions, while big companies and big unions have the power to make agreements that affect the welfare of consumers and weaker economic groups.

While many companies and unions have achieved a mature relationship characterized by mutual respect and broad understanding of the issues involved, this is not universally true. Indeed, there are areas of extreme antagonism and suspicion. Even those firms and unions that do get along well often indulge in flamboyant rhetoric that gives the appearance of real conflict. It is not, in short, easy to find out where justice lies in concrete cases.

ATTITUDES TOWARD UNIONS

The employer must recognize the fact that unions have a right to exist for the attainment of lawful objectives. Indeed, unions are a necessity. First, they supply the only reasonable method of working out bilateral agreements in those areas where unilateral agreements are unjust. Second, they provide a countervailing power that, at least in theory, should minimize some abuses.

Unfortunately, the history of unionism has seen the rise of many abusive practices and even collusion between management and labor against the interest of other parties in the economy. These abuses should not blind us to their essential legitimacy as well as the need for unions. Nor should they lead us to advocate measures that cure evils only by making it impossible, or at least difficult, for the unions to fulfill their necessary and useful functions. Sound attitudes, factual investigations, and discretion are obligations here as elsewhere in business life. If these are lacking in either the company manager or the union leader, the relationship will develop into a power struggle that will endanger all parties involved.

"RIGHT-TO-WORK" LAWS

The so-called right-to-work laws are actually laws that forbid management and labor to sign contracts providing for union or agency shops. The unions oppose them as union-busting laws. Certain business persons propose them as ways of protecting workers who do not want to join unions. The issues, however, cannot be understood without some background.

Any discussion of the right-to-work laws must start off with the fact that a recognized bargaining agent must, by law, operate in the interests of all people in the bargaining unit whether they be members of the union or not. This is a sound law, for if the unions won gains only for their members, we could soon have a situation in which two people with the same qualifications, doing the same job in the same plant, would receive quite different compensation. Basic equity, then, demands that a union bargain for all.

Bargaining and the processing of grievances are expensive. The union, by law, must bear this expense and so must protect its financial position. As a result, unions have invented a variety of contractual relationships with employers, designed either to maintain membership or at least protect their treasuries. So long as the contract is truly free, it is ethically valid, since it is in the public interest to maintain the union in a healthy condition.

It is objected that contracts requiring maintenance of membership, or the check-off of dues without membership, violate the right of the employee to a job. The *closed shop,* which requires an employer to hire only workers who are already union members, is ethically questionable as well as illegal since it gives the union control over job opportunities and permits them, in some cases, to artificially raise wages by controlling the supply of labor. The *union shop,* which requires an employee to become a union member within thirty days of employment, does not include the evils of the closed shop. It does not limit opportunities for employment nor take away the manager's right to employ those he or she thinks are best qualified. The same may be said of *agency shop* contracts in which an individual is not obliged to become a union member, but must pay dues to the union to cover the cost of representation. In the *open shop,* of course, employees are free not to join and need not pay even prorata assessments to the union.

The ethical question involved in the union shop and the checkoff may be phrased as follows: Are the limitations or conditions of employment an *unreasonable* interference with the freedom of a job applicant? We must remember that the applicant, if hired, will as a rule benefit from union activities. Simple equity would seem to say that the applicant has an obligation to pay his or her share of the expenses. For this reason a contract calling for a check-off or for ultimate union membership appears to be quite reasonable. The applicant's right to work is not impeded in any way. He or she is merely required to pay for the benefits the union is obliged to provide.

In some cases, it may be argued that the union shop and the check-off force the honest applicant to cooperate with crooks and undesirable people. This may well be the case, but the so-called "right to work" laws are not designed to cure the basic evils in the union itself. For this reason they are not reasonable legislation. Furthermore, the moral problem of the applicant who finds him or herself in a crooked union can be solved in a consideration of the principles covering cooperation. Finally, the individual should remember that business, too, often forces workers to cooperate with crooks and other undesirables. We do not feel this fact supports legislation that would force either business or unions to provide services without recompense.

Union busting and the systematic denigration of unions by outside propaganda should be avoided. This obligation springs not only from the demands of truthfulness and personal integrity but also from the fact that such propaganda creates defensive postures which break down good industrial relations. Worst of all, negative publicity is often used as a substitute for the creative solution that reconciles the legitimate interests of all parties.

SWEETHEARTS FOREVER

The "sweetheart" contract, which protects the interests of labor leaders and employers at the expense of workers and customers, is so obviously an unethical conspiracy that no further comment is needed. However, a word must be said about contracts that respect the right of the workers but harm the public good. The management that surrenders to union demands, with only a ritual show of bargaining because it can pass increased costs on to customers, is acting unethically. Power over prices, even though limited, does not absolve managers from the duty of protecting the interests of all who depend on them. Continued abuse in such situations normally leads to legislation. What is at stake, then, is the economic system and not merely wages and prices in a given situation. Much the same must be said of union-management cooperation in carving up markets, eliminating competition, and lobbying.

To put it simply, if it is unethical for the management to conspire with other companies for unethical purposes, it is equally unethical to cooperate with a union for the same purpose. Unions, after all, are not exempt from the demands of ethics.

This does not mean that management-labor disputes must never force others to pay higher prices. After all, the principle of proportionality applies here as elsewhere. The public has no right to low prices that are made possible only by the existence of inadequate wages. What is to be condemned is the disregard of the public interest and the use of power to attain inflated prices. Moreoever, since the line between the legitimate and the illegitimate can be difficult to determine, we are probably in need of some public guide line which has been worked out by all interested parties.

OTHER ABUSIVE PRACTICES

It should be obvious that the manager has a right, and often an obligation, to fight against union practices that encourage economic inefficiency, discrimination, and the limitation of the owner's right to communicate with his workers. Certain quota systems, featherbedding, and the slow-down are harmful not only to the firm but to the economy as a whole. At times there may be proportionate reasons for allowing such situations to continue. This only means that the immediate obligation is transformed into the obligation to work with trade associations and legislators for a long-range solution.

At this point, work on the ethics of unions is needed to clarify all the areas of management-union relations. There appears little need to develop the point, however, since like most human beings, managers are very aware of the unethical conduct of others. What must be stressed, however, is that management cannot silently connive forever. Excuses of a serious nature do exist, but they are not permanent justifications for the tolerance of evil.

CREATIVE ETHICS

While a certain amount of tension between management and union is good, there is an obligation to see that this tension does not injure the company or the economy. To achieve this goal, we need creative thinking rather than the senseless shouting of trite slogans. Although completely rational and impartial decisions may be impossible, it is irrational and immoral to surrender the field to the free play of power.

The creative process demands that both manager and union escape from their old frame of reference. The manager should realize that wages and fringe benefits are gradually becoming a part of their fixed costs. Law, unions, and public opinion will not tolerate wages being considered a cost that the manager may vary at will. Social Security, Unemployment Compensation, Seniority Rights, and the guaranteed annual wage are all expressions of this attitude. Other nations, such as Japan, already see wages as a fixed cost. There are disadvantages in this attitude, but such a view would certainly motivate business to work toward greater stability in production and toward a more efficient use of its work force.

Once again the point to be stressed is the idea that there is an obligation to change those aspects of reality that force us to give less than justice to others. This is a never-ending process and one which requires imagination and the ability to escape the curse of routine thinking. At the very least, it requires us to be open to new ideas that may improve both business and the ethical conduct of human affairs. In the long run, such attitudes are necessary for survival, since the forces of society will make the change if business does not. Changes made by others, of course, may not be sensitive to the exigencies of business.

Unions have become more and more sensitive to what affects the lives of workers as well as what affects their pocketbook. While union demands in noneconomic areas may threaten so-called management rights, it must be remembered that there is authority in the business firm that belongs to all members of the firm and need not be delegated to management. In addition, as the collective bargaining agreement has more and more implications for consumers and society at large, there will probably be demands for outside representation to protect outside rights. As labor relations become a public concern as a matter of fact, they will have to become a public concern as a matter of law.

THE LOCAL COMMUNITY

Business firms and the local communities in which they are located depend on one another. Their interests, however, are not identical, nor is their power equal except accidentally. There are cases where a single firm may dominate the economy and even the politics of an area. There are other cases where the community may look on a business as a friendly cow to be milked at will. Just as businesses compete for favorable local conditions, so communities compete for new firms that will bolster their tax bases and employment figures. Since politicans are not less human than business persons, there are even cases of sweetheart arrangements that line the pockets of owners and politicians without benefiting the community itself. At other times, the interests of a firm and a given community may coincide but be at odds with the interest of organized labor, of other communities, and of society as a whole.

As in the case of union-management relations, society has laws and principles that cover the more flagrant abuses such as political corruption. As yet, however, we have not developed an ethic to regulate the new relationships that have arisen with the passage of time and the changing nature of both the firm and the local community. Once again then, we are plunging into an area that requires further exploration.

POWER SHIFTS AND VALUES

Historically, individuals in business have nearly always occupied positions of power and influence in American communites. Sometimes they have used this power for purely personal aims, sometimes for the good of the entire community in which they took real pride. The same groups that formed the company towns and kept new business out lest it increase competition also built libraries and hospitals. Sometimes they perpetuated patterns of discrimination and segregation but, in many cases, they pushed for new schools. Though the picture is not completely one-sided, the locally-owned business was at least a part of the community. Its leaders shared common values and were as likely as not to be devoted to the place where they lived and worked.

Today, the pattern has changed. National firms with outside managers are a part of many communities, and these have not only power but interests that extend far beyond the local scene. In short, we are dealing with a modern form of the absentee landlord. This is not necessarily evil, since many large corporations are acutely aware of the need for community relations. On the other hand, real problems can develop from such issues as plant relocation and tax increases. What makes problems difficult is not merely the fact that there is great power (this existed even when plants were locally owned), but the fact that there is a lack of any ethical consensus as to what makes the good corporate citizen.

The community involvement of outside corporations is often good but superficial. Companies encourage membership in service organizations, but may frown on political involvement. Hard work in the Community Chest drive makes for real progress and a good public relations report, but it is no substitute for a fight against local corruption. Percentage contributions to local charities are laudable, but they do not make up for the failure to take a stand on racial integration in schools. At the same time, the large corporations may have good reasons for avoiding stands on more fundamental issues. It is a guest who does not want to offend a host, even though the host is relatively powerless. It fears that political involvement on the part of officers who only stay a few years will not really help the community to solve its own problems. In short, because we have no completely acceptable patterns of involvement, the firm may have to steer a fairly innocuous middle course. This, however, does not change the fact that the most talented people in the community are not really a part of its inner life.

While the problems mentioned above are real, they are not so crucial as those revolving around plant relocation and the use of natural resources, since decisions and policies in these areas can have a dramatic impact on both the present and the future of the local community. As we shall see, the impact that some businesses have on the environment can extend beyond the local community to society as a whole.

PLANT RELOCATION

A business cannot succeed without the help of the local community any more than the community can prosper without business. Because of this, continued association gives rise to a real, though vague and implied contract. Business normally expects that the local community will maintain a reasonable and orderly tax policy and encourage good labor relations. The community, on its side, assumes that business will strive to maintain stable employment patterns as well as pay its taxes and protect community resources. Although the contract between the firm and the community is not enforceable by law, it generates a real obligation on both sides, since orderly social life and community development are impossible without it.

At the same time, we must recognize the fact that both firm and community are only parts of large economic and social units that have overriding interests. A national or regional firm is responsible to workers, suppliers, and stockholders in many communities. Even a purely local firm is often responsible to customers who are spread over a broad geographical area. Business, as a result, cannot make its decisions purely in terms of the local community. There are, indeed, situations where the greater good demands relocation or severe curtailment of operations in a particular locality.

Relocation and curtailment of operations based on genuine economic factors will generally be ethical, although there are problems of method and manner. At the same time, we must recognize the fact that some relocations are motivated by the possibility of *exploiting* cheap labor in other areas, or by the chance to gain an economic advantage through political power. There are even cases on record where the move was dictated by the possibility of escaping a strong union. Because such factors do exist, there is some doubt as to whether or not firms should be allowed to make relocation decisions unilaterally. Inasmuch as the public interest is at stake, it has been suggested that firms should be forced to justify their decisions before a neutral body that would decide if the move was economically justifiable. As yet, thinking on this question is not very advanced, since this is another area where the traditional market forces do not necessarily guarantee true economic progress.

Even when the decision to relocate is justifiable, the method must be considered. In addition, consideration should be given to preventative measures that will minimize the possibility of relocation hurting communities in the future.

Many of the problems can be solved if a company has policies designed to prevent imbalances. Forward-looking companies, for example, avoid becoming the dominant employer in any one region, so that strong obligations based on dependency cannot develop. Such a policy prevents a company from sinking too much money into an area and so losing mobility.

If this balance has been established, the problem of plant relocation has been minimized. The idea of balance needs to be carried into the process of relocation itself so that harmful impacts are mitigated. The gradual phasing out of an operation gives an area time to prepare for adjustments by not upsetting the balance all at once. Cooperation with government, in retraining programs or in the relocation of workers, can further soften the blow.

Local communities, interested in maintaining economic stability, must do their part to foster it. In particular, they must encourage good labor relations and provide adequate community services. More concretely, they must see to it that local housing and schools are attractive and adequate lest firms have difficulty in recruiting competent people. In many cases, the community must also provide such educational facilities as will assure both trained workers and management to local industry. Unless the communities do their part, they may be responsible for making relocation necessary.

THE ENVIRONMENT

There is little argument that some businesses have exploited, and sometimes abused, the natural environment including animals and other nonhuman entities. Many firms have damaged the natural world, for example, by contributing to the depletion of several natural resources, marring mountains, rivers, and streams and by causing injury to and, in some cases, the extinction of some species of animals. Quite often the side effects of production have come to pose serious threats to human health and safety.

Some industries, among them the extractive, chemical, and fuel or power generating types, and also the transportation business along with numerous manufacturing concerns, have significantly contributed to what has commonly come to be referred to as the "environmental crisis." It is now clear that such unreflective and often exploitive treatment of the environment not only threatens human health and safety, but also has negative effects on the economic stability of society and the extent to which human beings are able to live in harmony with nature, their fellows, and their own inner or spiritual being. Finding itself facing rising levels of air, water, and noise pollution and increasing instances of business-caused damage to the earth, and various other natural objects, society has come to demand that many businesses take clearer account of the effects of their activities on nature and on human health.

The first, quite normal response on the part of society to the environmental crisis has been motivated by self-interest rather than by an interest in or concern for nature itself.[1] Given, for example, pollution of the water table, permanent damage to the ozone layer, the many instances of careless disposal of toxic wastes and hazardous chemicals, and indiscreet uses of dangerous pesticides, in the interest of human health and survival, society has endeavored to enjoin business to clean up the environment. Under the pressure of society's proclamation that it will no longer surrender human health to profit and will no longer pay for what many businesses have long considered to be the external

[1]See James A. Keller, "Types of Motives for Ecological Concern," *Zygon*, Vol. 6, no. 3, Sept. 1971, pp. 197–209, for an interesting discussion on motives for ecological concern. We will, in fact, make some use of his fundamental distinction among such motives to provide a framework from within which to analyze the motives of business and society in regard to concern for the environment. Keller tends to support a modified form of altruism as the proper motive for ecological concern over, what he calls, crass self-interest and enlightened self-interest.

costs of production, businesses will have to take a more responsible position in their treatment of the natural world.

There has been some significant change of attitude regarding the environment, in recent years, on the part of several industries. For example, the large paper manufacturing companies now tend to plant more trees each year than they cut down, and mining companies are finally taking a more complete account of the costs of land reclamation. While these efforts reflect a measure of ecological consciousness on the part of business and are at the same time quite beneficial to society, such ecological concern is nonetheless founded on self-interest as well.

Many corporations assume responsibility for care of the environment because, for example, prudence suggests that addressing problems of deforestation and soil erosion at the present time will, in all likelihood, be more cost-effective than doing so in the future. Prudence also suggests that the failure of business to take its responsibility for proper treatment of the environment will result in severe and, perhaps excessive, regulation of business activities.

Society will, in the end, specify the ecological obligations of business. That society, rather than business, should do this is necessary for two reasons. First, if industries contributing to an environmental problem police themselves, the more scrupulous, ecologically conscious firms may put themselves at a competitive disadvantage as the prices of their products rise. Second, and perhaps more important, the health of the environment (no less than the physical well-being of the society), is a social obligation. After all, the relationship between business and society is a contractual one, and implied in this social contract is the notion that the vast natural resources of society have been entrusted to business in order that the overall welfare of society should be preserved. While the determination of business obligations regarding treatment of the environment will ultimately be a societal one initially founded on self-interest, businesses also, out of self-interest and by having a right, must be encouraged to participate in this determination lest they be overrun.

It should be noted that the above line of argument—that each business and society, as a whole, must be encouraged to take up more ecological concern, at least initially, out of self-interest—is necessarily founded on the presumption that the environment has no intrinsic worth or value in its own right. Such a position, therefore, entails seeing nature as an object, wholly instrumental in character, or as having value merely as a means to exclusively human ends and purposes. We must recall that the environmental crisis was brought upon us, in large measure, by self-interest. While businesses, in their quest for profit, were the bigger contributors to the crisis, society was not blameless, as it often desired convenience and luxury.

Such ecological concern, motivated primarily by self-interest, however justified, and fueled by the presumption that nature has only instrumental value, has caused some individuals to wonder if nature will continue to be exploited in the absence of some higher and, perhaps, more objective motivation for ecological concern. Out of what might be described as a sense of altruism, some individuals—and at the present time the number is growing—have taken an interest in preserving and protecting the environment because they attribute value to the natural entities "in and of themselves," whether they are nonhuman or natural objects. That is to say, these individuals hold the position that nature has a value in itself, a value not bestowed on nature by humankind. This altruistic ecological attitude is ultimately a reaction against most forms of ecological concern motivated by self-interest.

The more extreme form of altruism as a motive for ecological concern has manifested itself in various theoretical and practical endeavors to establish rights for nonhuman, or natural objects (for example, rivers, trees, oceans, mountains), and including animals. We may see a time in the future when this sort of altruistic ecological concern, founded on a genuine respect for nature and its creatures, will initiate legislative changes that, if not actually demanding the attribution of rights to animals and other natural objects, will serve to guarantee nonhuman entities more substantial protection under the law. However, it seems unlikely that businesses can continue to flourish under increasingly rigid contraints regarding the rights of natural objects. We expect that an overemphasis on the rights of such nonhuman entities will, in the long run, put burdensome demands on business and on society as a whole. It is agreed that there are many serious moral dilemmas regarding treatment of animals presently facing, for example, the meat producing, and fur and hide industries. However, cost/benefit analyses will ultimately show that, in the advanced industrial society, technology-bound as it is, productivity would be severely challenged under the strain of such rights' claims. In the same way that unreasonable demands by society for safety in products would not prove beneficial in the long-run, so too will unrealistic claims attributing unconditional value to the environment and nonhuman natural entities prove to be economically infeasible. The bottom line is that society will, in all probability, be unwilling to bear the expense of guaranteeing such rights for nature and natural objects. Clear cut and defensible rights for natural objects will only become a reality when society goes through an extraordinarily radical, and in our judgment highly unlikely, 360 degree turn of attitude regarding the treatment of nonhuman entities.

Midway between rather narrow self-interest and altruism can be discerned a third type of motive for ecological concern, which is used by individuals who have argued that the environmental crisis should be taken seriously. This motive has been termed "enlightened self-interest." It is admitted that when enlightened self-interest is the motivation for ecological concern, nature still has no intrinsic value. While nature does not have value in and of itself, it does, however, have aesthetic and even spiritual value. Enlightened self-interest allows us to see nature as having a heightened or more noble utility. Nature is beautiful, awesome, inspiring, and sublime. The natural world, then, is valued as beautiful, yet not independent of human appreciation. Nature is sublime or beautiful insofar as humans attribute such sublimity or beauty to it. Consequently, having ecological concern out of enlightened self-interest is somewhat similar to having concern for nature out of altruism, at least in the sense that both motives presume a value in nature and the environment that transcends narrow or crass utility. Presumed, rather, is a deferential and reverential disposition toward the natural world and its creatures.

Enlightened self-interest, as a motivation for ecological concern, is of course similar to more or less material self-interest in that both motives are founded on the assumption that nature has value in terms of the contribution it can make to human development and to human goals and purposes. The difference, however, between these motives lies in the character of the use to which nature is put in each. Very simply, the individuals who take up ecological concern founded on enlightened self-interest assume that nature contributes to the human condition in a higher, more noble sense. The claim is that a life lived in harmony with nature is more fulfilling, in effect, more human and "that man loses something when he misuses nature; what he loses is aesthetic or spiritual; it touches his heart and his innermost being."[2]

As technology comes to occupy a greater and greater place in our lives, and as the natural environment changes and is changed in the name of what we imagine to be social progress, we run the risk of losing sight of the fact that "wonder" is an essential characteristic of the human being. Nature has long been the inspiration for humankind's moments of glorious insight and flights of spirit. To debase nature is at the same time to debase ourselves. To diminish our opportunities to enjoy, commune with, and live at peace in the natural world is, perhaps, at the same time to cut off access to our own sense of wonderment, to that which makes us most human.

Business has the capacity and opportunity to effect significant change in the environment, to alter nature itself. Business, as always, has the minimum moral obligation not to harm society, in this case by exploiting or abusing the environment and thus perhaps endangering the health of the members of society. Moreover, granting economical and technological feasibility even in the absence of a clear societal mandate, business should take up ecological concern out of a sense of enlightened self-interest in an effort to serve more than the material needs of society.

As we have seen throughout this book, business can affect the manner and the degree to which human beings are able to live in harmony with their fellows and with their own inner being and conscience. Now, it might be suggested that the extent to which we can all exist in harmony with the natural world in the future depends, in large measure, on the overall attitude that business takes toward profit making, production, and the development of technology. If we are to have a livable environment and are to be allowed the full

[2]Keller, p. 199.

expression of our rationality, our freedom, and our sense of wonder toward our humanity, business must produce goods and make a profit in ways consistent with the protection and preservation of the natural world.

BY WAY OF SUMMARY

Whether the firm is dealing with the union or with the local community, or whether, in its activities, it is affecting the environment, it should remember that neither power nor custom can justify its actions. The world has changed; technology has in some ways generated more problems than it can solve, and business persons must become aware of such change in the world if they are to act ethically and efficiently. Because the world changes, it is difficult, if not impossible, to catalogue all of the problems that can arise. Three points, however, should be clear. First, the manager should be sensitive to the actual and potential impacts of his or her acts. Second, he or she should seek cooperation rather than conflict as a means of solving problems that arise in relationships with groups having unequal power. This cooperation should not take the form of a conspiracy, which exploits unrepresented third parties, but should look for the creative solution that, by rising above the traditional and known, finds a level where all interests can be more perfectly harmonized. At times, it may even involve legislation that will protect honest companies and third parties from power plays and politics. Finally, the way businesses treat the environment in the future—the party long unrepresented—may, in fact, be one measure of the business community's coming-of-age.

Although some will say that these suggestions disregard the true nature of business, we believe that they indicate what business will be and must be if it is to fulfill its mission. Equally important, they indicate the challenge and satisfaction that business people can gain if they see their work in a broader perspective. Indeed, as we shall see in the final chapter, the new mission of the business person may involve changed attitudes towards the whole of the economy and the world itself.

14

BUSINESS AND THE SOCIAL ECONOMY

INTRODUCTION

The preceding chapters have raised issues of social importance and posed problems that cannot be completely solved by individual firms, or even by the business community as a whole. It is time, then, to take a look at the ethical problems of the business system itself. While there is not room for a full treatment, a glance at even a few issues will help to clarify the ethical challenge that faces business in the twentieth century.

Ethics is concerned with judging the suitability of the means to the end. If the means does not serve the end, or serves it at too high a cost, we cannot ethically continue to use it. Moreover, if there are alternative means that serve the end with less cost, that is, with fewer harmful side effects, good ethics obliges us to abandon our present course of action. Our business system, like the Constitution of the United States, or even a system of family organization, is a means, not an end. It is neither a sacred cow nor an ultimate value. It is a tool to be reevaluated in terms of the goals it is supposed to serve. The system itself is controlled by firms, and the firms by individuals. In the last analysis, people must do the evaluating and make the changes necessary to bring the system more closely into line with the changing needs of human beings and the society of which they are a part. As we have noted again and again, this responsibility cannot be avoided, although often it is transformed into the duty of doing what can be done at a given moment. After all, there can be no excuse for not looking at things as they are rather than as we would like to believe they are.

THE PARADOXES OF THE AMERICAN ECONOMY

We live in the richest nation in the history of the world. Our gross national product staggers the imagination even as it continues to grow. Both our per capita and average family income are so high that other nations appear to live in abject poverty. We have extraordinary conveniences and luxuries; and yet we live in a nation where poverty and, more often than we realize, even deprivation continue to exist on a fairly broad scale.

The existence of this poverty is paradoxical, since we have excess capacity and idle manpower in both agriculture and business. Indeed, the very efficiency of our economy and the brilliance of our technological advances help to create poverty by making workers obsolete at the same time that they create new goods to satisfy human needs. Strangely enough, people are often in the position where they can buy luxuries, such as a television set, but cannot get necessities, such as good housing. It must be admitted that some children who live in good homes must go to substandard schools. Moreover, anyone who has traveled in Europe will admit that our cities lack much of the charm and beauty one would expect to find in a wealthy nation. The traveler who has visited Holland, Sweden, or Switzerland will also have to confess that there is nothing in those countries to equal our rows of slums, which are like great unsanitary prisons.

In point of fact, then, the United States appears to have refused to use its resources to satisfy the private and public needs of its citizens. It has made progress, to be sure, but the system has not really used its riches to good advantage. This failure cannot be explained except by saying that we have refused to admit the problem and have hesitated to attack it with full vigor.

HIDING THE PROBLEM

Although social critics have publicized problems for generations, the general public has not always faced them. Many never have any contact with poverty, since it is found in geographic and racial pockets. Others who do meet it face-to-face often reinterpret it to suit their convenience. Thus, poverty is interpreted to be either a temporary state, which will disappear, or the result of indolence. In addition, the picture of the good life is so well publicized by advertisements that there is little room left for news of poverty except at Thanksgiving and Christmas.

Our public poverty is easier to disguise. Most of our people have limited ways of comparing their present state to something better. Indeed, even our better-educated people are sometimes very poor judges of the quality of the education being given to their children. If you are used to ugly cities, it is difficult to criticize them. If you are used to thinking of your public services as the best in the world, it is impossible to realize that they may be very poor indeed.

Even when we have admitted the existence of such problems as poverty, we have not faced them. We have been persuaded that time will work things out. We have been told that government intervention is too expensive or too dangerous. We have been convinced, in fact, that the world is really all right despite appearances to the contrary. The Great Depression of the thirties dispelled many of these ideas, and the nation made some progress, since it was realized that the ordinary mechanics of business and the competitive system could not solve all problems. This, however, was crisis activity, and the old mentality has continued to blind us to many problems.

THE MYTH OF COMPETITION

Not only the existence and nature of poverty, but the true nature of our economic system are mysteries to a large part of our population, including a large part of the business community itself. Many small businesses do exist in a world of rather real competition, in which no one seller can really influence prices or the allocation of resources. Since there are a number of these businesses, both their owners and friends constitute a large group believing in the existence of a kind of competition that automatically assures that justice is done. Such ideas are, of course, reinforced by superficial courses in economics as well as by Fourth of July orations and the publications of the National Association of Manufacturers.

Students of the economy, of course, have been well aware that the small business does not set the tone of the economy. Big business does that, and big business has had the power to escape much of the discipline of the market. As a result, it has often been able to set prices and allocate capital in a way that was not envisaged by classic economic theory. These very groups have an interest in maintaining the myth of competition, since this helps to quiet the nerves of the populace. They have even coined such misleading terms as "people's capitalism" in order to turn attention from the real centers of power in the economy. This fact of tremendous power in large concerns is generally concealed by another set of slogans that extol free enterprise, the American system, and other vague but emotionally attractive concepts.

This fact of power must be acknowledged by the individual. One must be aware of the influence of economic concentration on the political and public sphere. The political influence that big business exerts is not merely the result of political contributions and memberships on government committees. It also rests on the work of lobbies, which do a good and not necessarily dishonest job of representing the business position to Congress.

Big business and its trade associations are aided by small business in protecting the public mind from contamination by reality. There are committees that scan school books to make sure that they do not deviate too much from the picture business wants to present. There are foundations that run programs for clergymen in the hope of teaching them a simple and favorable picture of the economy. There are newsletters available to educators that further inculcate a simplified and comforting picture of the system. We cannot say exactly how effective all of these efforts are. However, we find that the old myths are pretty well embedded in the thinking of our students and even in the economic philosophy of many college professors.

We do not wish to imply that business people are either vicious or stupid in fostering these myths. Many of them are true believers who have never stopped to question the system. Others are so busy that they do not have the time to examine the reality of the world in which they live. Still others feel that they are only countervailing forces struggling against the unions, the reformers, and cryptosocialists. Our point is merely that we must face reality and discover if it is really serving our goals.

THE TRANSCENDENTAL MARGIN

The myths of universal affluence and of the competitive system are reinforced by the idea that our economic progress, limited though it is, has been due to a business system that is profit motivated. This, to be sure, is the major reason for not rocking the boat or criticizing the goose-that-laid-the-golden egg. In point of fact, however, much of our progress, not only in production but in the just distribution of economic goods, has been due to the modifications that we have made in the system and in what Berle calls the *transcendental margin.*[1]

> The transcendental margin is the product of a value system that causes effort and expenditure beyond that calculated as conducive to the personal advantage of an individual or his or her immediate family group.
>
> Development occasioned by such a value system does not exclude, but rather includes, use of the state and its agencies in mobilizing and applying effort and expenditure. But its effect is never limited to state measures and actions. The aggregate of such effort, expenditure, and sacrifice, over and above the aggregate and expenditure for such personal desires, is the added coefficient that causes the national product to increase beyond satisfying the aggregate effective personal desires of the population.

These statements mean that the United States has improved both the productivity of its economy and the distribution of its wealth by devoting much of its resources to areas outside the profit-motivated economy. They mean that we have used gifts, foundations, and private organizations of a not-for-profit status to improve the lot of human beings and, indirectly, the efficiency of the productive machine. They mean that the government has increasingly been a factor in production as well as in redistribution.

[1]Adolph A. Berle, *The American Economic Republic* (New York: Harcourt, Brace & World, 1963), p. 202.

Many people do not want to face these facts, for they show that an increase in non-market activity and a decrease in market power may be the clue to progress. Worse yet, they may indicate that all of the propaganda against these changes may be a real disservice to the nation and even to the economic side of business.

PROFITS AND SOCIAL COSTS

If we accept the fact that both growth and progress have stemmed from a mixed system, it follows that profit may be a meaningless concept to use in the evaluation of the social performance of a firm or of the business sector of the economy. When much of the productivity is due to the results of education, profit may represent the surplus created by society rather than by the business system, or it may be that profits can be viewed as money that the firm did not expend because it did not pay all operating costs. Smog, industrial odors, pollution of rivers, shortened lives, and nervous tension are all costs of production paid by society and private individuals, even though they are not shown clearly on the balance sheet of any corporation.

Social costs are represented not only by the scars of strip mining and the still active underground mine fire which threatens to destroy a town, but, in a different vein, by the actual effects on the family and the education of the children of both parents working. As we have already mentioned, the traveling husband, for example, who may not be able to fulfill his duty as father completely, may also represent a social cost. We do not know exactly what business does cost us nor what it gives us. Perhaps we can never know with complete accuracy, but we must make some attempt to find out if we are to evaluate the system as it is and not as it is imagined to be.

ECONOMIC DISLOCATION AND STABILITY

Some time ago the United States decided that the cost of instability was too high and adopted government measures designed to mitigate fluctuations and their effects on workers. The work of the Federal Reserve in balancing credit, the effects of unemployment compensation on dropping purchasing power, and federal aid to depressed areas are all designed to reduce the cost of the free-market system. Urban renewal programs have also helped in improving housing when the private economy proved incapable of doing the job in time. Business people are not always happy about these plans, which limit their freedom and their power in many ways, but most will admit that the programs have benefited both business and the general society. The question remains, however, as to whether or not we have done all that we can to reduce the cost of instability without harming the essential mechanisms of a free society. Do we need to stabilize the use of consumer credit which has been responsible at least in part for some of our recessions? Do we need to extend the coverage of unemployment insurance? Do we need a hundred other measures to control inflationary forces which benefit the debtor but impoverish those with fixed incomes?

The problems of instability are being compounded by dislocations resulting from changing markets, changing technology, and the resulting cultural lag. The blessings of technology are liable to bring us new unemployment at the same time that they obsolete equipment and increase our over-capacity. The new economy is demanding new skills at a rate that is quickly outstripping society's ability to train workers. Plant relocations to meet new markets and to take advantage of lower labor costs can leave whole communities gasping for life. All of this takes place in a nation that already has depressed areas and a considerable body of unemployed and poor. As yet, we have not developed a way of attacking these problems on a global and continuous basis. The costs of dislocation are high, and we must ask if the system needs to be readjusted to reduce them.

NEW CONCEPTS AND NEW VALUES

Advanced technology creates the possibility that more and more goods will be produced with less and less manpower. If anything, it will aggravate the problem of abundance, since the increase in production creates a problem in distribution. Even business persons recognize the fact that increased capacity may be self-defeating unless income is so distributed that large numbers can buy the new fruits of the business system. At this point, the attempts at a solution are complicated by the problems of definition and evaluation which, while they may seem very abstract and philosophic, must be solved if we are to act intelligently.

The business person would like to solve the problem of excess capacity and abundance by teaching people to fill their new leisure with consumption. *Consumption is thus elevated to the status of a virtue*, if not a patriotic duty. Others, however, see leisure as the time a human being can use to be a human being with or without consumption. These thinkers see the possibility of an age in which people have time to cultivate the mind and the spirit as adults and not merely while they are children in school. They see the possibility of increasing unpaid services in areas where there is real need. *Consumption is no virtue* for these and may even be a vice if it keeps human beings from doing more important things.

A change in our concepts of the nature and value of leisure involves a change in our idea of work. If leisure, or time during which we have a chance to be human, is more important than consumption, then work becomes not so much a means of earning a living and buying things, as a means of transforming the world and developing one's own personality. In such a world, an individual would not be judged by how much he or she has, but by what sort of person this individual is and by how much this person contributed to society. A change in our concept of work and leisure would involve a change in evaluation that would relegate the entire business system to a less important place in our society. This is not pure theory, for many societies, some of them rich and highly cultivated, have adopted a similar point of view.

Business people are not used to thinking in such philosophic terms, for they are people of action. Yet action is guided by our values and not merely by blind urges. In the last analysis, it is our idea of the good life and the value of the individual that controls everything that can be controlled. It seems to us, then, that ultimately business may have to face the problem of ascertaining the relative values and meaning of work, leisure, and consumption.

RELATIONS WITH GOVERNMENT

Although the deeper issues raised above cannot be solved by any one agency, it should be obvious that many of the questions can be answered only in terms of a new form of cooperation between business and government. This relationship has grown in time and will continue to grow both in extension and intensity. This is necessary, for we are in a time of transition. It is also inevitable, for as economic power increases, the relationship between it and political power becomes more and more crucial. It has been argued, and in our judgment correctly, that the problem cannot be solved merely by deciding on the proper and exclusive field of each power. The two spheres interact, as they must.

Up to the present time, business has often insisted on viewing government as an enemy. The business person fails to admit that any good can come out of Washington, lest the position of business is compromised. Instead of entering into rational discourse with the government and society as a whole, businesspeople often hope for a sort of high school debate which aims not at the truth but at victory. While the interest of business and government may not always coincide completely, the continuance of warfare or, at best, heavily armed neutrality will not solve the problem.

When the business person does enter the political arena, it is all too often as a politician who would manipulate the machinery of government for selfish purposes. Only a few have adopted a statesman-like posture and looked for creative solutions. These are hard words, but the ideas have been drawn not so much from the enemies of business as from the thoughtful writings of individuals within its own ranks.

If business people are to make a full contribution to society, they must first realize that they are no longer the simple hucksters who are tolerated, if not despised, but rather, members of the new aristocracy. It may be an aristocracy of power, money, and intelligence, but it is still guided by the principle of noblesse oblige. The obligations are not always easy to define, but a few examples will illustrate some areas where we believe they do exist.

LOBBYING

Lobbying is, in general, not only a legitimate but a necessary activity in our country. Unless legislators are carefully informed of the facts and of various points of view in a given society, they cannot legislate wisely. Truthful, informative lobbying should be encouraged. Lobbying, however, conjures up images of bribery, conspiracy, and pressure as well as the use of phony front organizations and various forms of blackmail. The unethical quality of most of these acts is so clear as to need no commentary. Indeed, the major problem may not exist in these areas at all.

The real difficulty is probably in the non-creative nature of much lobbying. Often, where there is a real political problem, business seems to be concerned not so much with helping to solve the problem, as with maintaining the status quo or receiving special protection. As a result, necessary social reforms are often neglected while business generally ends up in a worse position than it would have been with a truly creative solution. When lobbies are used for such purposes, one has doubts about business ethics even though the offense cannot be nicely classified in traditional ethical categories.

We have often been surprised to find people of good will lobbying against bills designed to remedy real abuses simply because these individuals possessed an inherent dislike of government, or because less honorable individuals had made it unpopular to support virtue publicly. Often, to be sure, the people of good will feel that self-regulation can do the job since they charitably endow others with their own integrity. Perhaps, it is merely an unconscious fear that the admission of some faults in the industry will encourage others to denigrate business and to supply unfair critics with ammunition. No matter what the explanation, the refusal to cooperate for a higher good is hardly the stand of the good citizen who realizes that there are times when personal advantage must be sacrificed to a higher end.

Our point can be made by relating a brief and simple story that exemplifies the opposition of business not only to the unreasonable portions of legislation on packaging, in this case, but to any legislation, even though it might help business itself. As the story goes, an executive in an important packaging firm attacked some packaging legislation, although he could not specify one objectional provision in it. He impressed his audience with the irrationality of his position and left them with the suspicion that he had not studied the legislation at all. It is this sort of opposition that hurts both business and society.

A similar lack of cooperation is sometimes found when the Federal Trade Commission asks for aid in developing standard terminology. As well as serving to police borderline operators, the development of trade guides can help and protect the honest manufacturer and retailer.

Honesty forces one to admit that the government sometimes has too many officials who are bent on crusades and on making a name for themselves. Often too, one can detect a note of hostility and a lack of understanding of the business person's problems. Some agencies leave major points so vague that business people do not know where they stand. Others are tempted to use detailed blueprints where none are required. It would appear that before we can make real progress in this area, there will be need for an ethic of government. The problem, however, will not be solved by continuing to accept the present relationship as definitive.

PLANNING

Many of the real problems in the American economy cannot be solved without cooperative planning in which government, business, and consumers have a role. Yet planning is an unsavory socialistic word to many business people. This is paradoxical, since business people are experts in planning and build their future on careful study and organization. Why, then, do they object to introducing the same rationality into the economic system as a whole?

To some extent, the opposition springs from a fear of government. Moreover, because planning would change the public meaning of profits, it might be feared that the glory, if not the challenge would be stolen from those in business. Profits, after all, are supposed to be not only a sign of success of having met the challenge of the market but also a justification of business power. To put it another way, business people may recognize that planning involves not merely increased efficiency and government intervention but a change in the meaning of business and in their own status.

It must be admitted, however, that planning is increasing elsewhere in the world and with considerable success. Actually, our own economy is already characterized by a great deal of planning and seems to have profited from it. Planning, moreover, does not mean government control, but cooperation with government. At best, it is the systematic study of means and ends. As such, it can even be consistent with free enterprise, although not, of course, with laissez faire or rugged individualism. In many cases, it involves the presentation of information and the use of persuasion in order to perfect the working of the market. It can thus leave the essential outlines of existing institutions relatively untouched in many cases.

While national planning is done under the auspices of the government, the control group can and does include representatives of business, the public, and the union, so that the will of the people will be more perfectly reflected in the choice of goals. The execution of those goals, however, must still be left to managers.

Although it is difficult to assess the success of planning in the non-Communist world, even conservative economists admit that it has not restrained progress. At the very least, plans seem to create an atmosphere of confidence, which promotes innovation and risk-taking. In many cases, plans have helped business to reduce the number of contradictory government policies and even to anticipate technical, material, and labor shortages in particular fields. Planning may also help to cut down investments that might lead to excess capacity.

While it may be impossible to take a definitive stand at this time, it seems difficult to imagine an America that cannot utilize the best of planning without sacrificing its basic values, even though some of the old folkways may have to be eliminated. Indeed, we suspect that even on the rational level, our national genius can equal, if not surpass, that of the French, the Germans, and the Swedes, who have done a great deal with far fewer resources than we enjoy.

INTERNATIONAL BUSINESS AND MULTINATIONAL CORPORATIONS

The emergence of the multinational corporation has stirred up a heated debate about the impact on the international economy and on the economies of developing nations. In order to understand the debate, it is useful to appreciate the motives of the multinationals and the benefits they bring to and the costs they impose on host countries.

Of the many reasons corporations become multinational it is often agreed that the following are among the most important: 1.) to gain tax advantages; 2.) to secure a cheap and plentiful labor force; 3.) to expand their market; 4.) to avoid strict regulations in the home country, for example, environmental regulations. All of these reasons are sound from a business or purely economic perspective. However, such motivations for doing business can also lead to abuses in the host country.

Some multinationals will locate themselves in foreign countries to gain tax breaks. However, it has been argued that many corporations achieve such tax-exempt status at substantial expense to the host country. The point is that even though the multinational may make extensive use of roads, harbors, and airports, the construction and maintenance of such things are paid for out of the revenues garnered from the quite often poverty-stricken general population.

On the other side of this coin, corporations often argue, is a fair trade-off. That is to say, the presence of the corporation in such a country will, in the long-run, be a tremendous benefit for the local and national economy. To a certain extent, this is true. Increased productivity should create more jobs, thus fueling, especially, the local economy by giving community members more spending power. Moreover, in the larger picture, the hoped for transfer of and education about technology from the multinational to the host country will help a developing country to become technologically more sophisticated and independent.

The creation of jobs is a clear benefit for the local economy as long as the wages paid the local workers are just. Unfortunately we have heard many stories where foreign employees have been exploited by multinationals in regard to wages and/or working conditions. In some circumstances, even if wages are fair (that is, reasonably comparable to similar wages in the home operation), or even quite high in comparison to local standards, there can occur indirect but nonetheless negative consequences. The presence of the multinational could offer damaging competition to essential indigenous productive processes. For example, some farmers may give up producing food to work in the plant that makes irons, or clothing, or clocks. Thus, less food is produced locally.

While it is true that the manufacturing concern may boost the local economy, it may only supply increased spending power for a small percentage of the community. In a severely poverty-stricken area, local merchants who perceive falsely that the standard of living is increasing and that more money can be made might raise prices for essentials thus injuring the poorer majority. Finally, the creation of an "upper poorer class" (that is, higher-income working class), can serve to generate conflict and cause social discord in the community.

There is no doubt that productivity and the development of techology will be central factors in aiding the progress of developing nations. These factors are often first introduced and further developed by multinational corporations, and the road to technological sophistication and independence has been paved many times by international business. However, education about technology and the sale or transfer of technologies to developing nations have, on occasion, been motivated by self-interest on the part of these corporations. There have been instances of corporations, for example, in the agricultural machinery and technology industries, selling near useless equipment to third world countries, useless because of geography, climate, lack of education, and the availability of necessary natural and economic resources to make such machinery work. The argument that multinationals can assist in helping to industrialize and supply technology to developing nations in, for example, Africa, Asia, and Latin America only holds if the technology supplied is truly useful and beneficial to the developing nation and not sold simply to satisfy the narrow interest of corporate profitability. A marriage of profit to the company and benefit to the customer is of course to be encouraged. But even a pressing financial need to expand a market, whether it be in industrial equipment or in commodities, is not sufficient justification to abuse the host country and its citizens.

It was in the interest of expanding their market in infant formula that the Nestle Corporation launched its massive promotion in a number of third-world nations. The case has been very widely publicized because of the highly questionable nature of the promotion in terms of advertising and public relations and because of the seriousness of the actual consequence of the campaign. Many infant deaths, it is claimed, were caused by inferior or contaminated formula and by negligence on the part of Nestle regarding its obligations to educate and supply adequate information to mothers in the third world using the formula in place of breast milk.

While expansion of a market into foreign countries, where regulations on commodities are not as rigid as they are in the home country, cannot serve as justification in itself for unethical practices by multinationals for these foreign nations—and of course expanding a market need not entail such abuses—neither can interest in avoiding strict environmental regulations allow multinationals to perpetuate abuses on the natural world in other parts of the globe. Proper care of the environment, nature as such, in whatever part of the world is a matter of individual and social justice. (See section on the environment, pp. 142–146.) Businesses have no less an obligation to operate in such a way as to preserve the health and safety of human beings and to respect nature, as such, in its own nation than it does in other nations across the globe.

Abuses abroad by U.S. multinationals, especially over the last decade, have generated increased interest on the part of society in regulating their international activities. It is now common knowledge, for example, that hundreds of corporations, including many of the Fortune 500 class, have given hundreds of millions of dollars in bribes to foreign governments. The Lockheed Corporation alone paid twelve million dollars in bribes to high ranking Japanese government officials to help market their TritStar plane. Such heightened societal interest ultimately gave birth to the Foreign Corrupt Practices Act of 1977, an act designed to control and/or eliminate payments (that is, bribes) made by U.S. corporations to officials abroad in order to secure business in these foreign countries.

It is apparent that such extravagant payments as those made by Lockheed offer immediate threats to the competitive system of international business. For example, the richer corporations are at a clear and unfair advantage in the competitive game. However, it has been argued that too much emphasis and overly harsh requirements regarding the control and elimination of "grease" payments might lead to severe economic losses and perhaps produce negative consequences for foreign relations. There is clearly a difference between large-scale bribery and smaller gift or grease payments to encourage bureaucrats and minor clerks or administrators to do their jobs. A few hundred dollars to expedite receiving a surverying permit, a sum quite often factored into the foreign government employee's salary, might be required to even begin the business venture. Even the Foreign Corrupt Practices Act does not *clearly prohibit* such payments.

Prohibition of these latter sorts of payments would result from our taking inadequate account of cultural differences, local customs, difference in morality, or norms and standards which bear not only on the proper product of business but also on the proper conduct of life. Lest the long-proclaimed U.S. imperialism raise its ugly head too often, we must be more accepting, tolerant, and reasonable about local practices, as long as such practices do not lead to extortion on a large scale. With the persistence of such extortion, the interests of the multinational, and its home business community, and the interests of the host country's business community would both suffer. Because, in all likelihood, other corporations than U.S. corporations will continue to bribe, U.S. companies will very often find themselves at a competitive disadvantage. Among the serious concerns here are loss of business abroad and given such loss of business, possibly loss of jobs at home. There can, of course, be political ramifications to multinational business practice as well, in that unreflective indifference to foreign business practices could serve to put a strain on foreign relations between the home and host countries.

Earlier in this section on multinational business it was suggested that these conglomerates sometimes victimize host nations and their citizens. However, it must be noted that host nations sometimes do the same to the multinationals. A large number of bribes paid by big multinationals to foreign political officials are extorted by these officials. In the same way that large-scale bribing to gain an unfair advantage threatens the competitive system and the integrity of business, so does extortion. In this sense, multinationals sometimes become victims as well.

A heightened and publicly proclaimed moral sensitivity by multinationals to corrupt business practices abroad can serve as a symbolic gesture of commitment by business to reduce business and political corruption, as such, in this country. It can also be a symbolic gesture to the rest of the world and to the international business community as well.

It must, however, not be forgotten that the multinational is, in some ways, beyond patriotism. It is often a corporate citizen of the world whose interests are broader than those of the nation state. While this extra-nationalism poses problems, it also provides opportunities for a push towards the formation of greater economic interdependence of nations, which in its turn can promote cultural interchange, effective cooperation, and an erosion of old hostilities. The European Common Market, it might be argued, has done more for the cause of peace than a thousand years of treaty making. Perhaps wittingly or unwittingly multinationals will play a similar role by creating business people without a country who draw nations into interdependence—union by the bonds of shared economic life. While this may sound idealistic, we should never lose sight of the fact that the merchant and peddler often spread civilization farther and faster than did the missionary.

IN CONCLUSION

This final chapter has probably left some readers bewildered and other readers angry. It is not practical, in the sense of being narrowly pragmatic. It may be condemned by some for it questions existing institutions and labels. Nevertheless this chapter is a necessary part of any book on business ethics that is not concerned with mere regulations but rather with the development of the creative function of business as a part of the broader society. Anyone with imagination will see that the realization of these ideas presents a challenge to the business community. Business is asked to see itself as a part of the mainstream of American life with something more important to contribute than what appears on a balance sheet.

The writers hope that business will undertake this significant task, for it alone has the techniques and knowledge necessary to translate such ideals into realities. Indeed, in the measure that business does meet the challenge, we can expect to find that our nation prospers and our freedom grows providing an inspiration to the rest of the world.

BIBLIOGRAPHY

A BIBLIOGRAPHICAL NOTE

A very good general source of information on publications in business ethics is Kenneth M. Bond, *Bibliography of Business Ethics and Business Moral Values,* copyright 1982, by Kenneth M. Bond, Omaha, Nebraska: Creighton University.

Bond has compiled extensive references to periodical articles, books, and collected works that deal with issues in business ethics. His bibliography also contains a list of other bibliographies of material on business ethics and citations of two syllabi collections. These are: Dill, Donaldson, et al., *Syllabi for the Teaching of Management Ethics* (Society for Values in Higher Education, 363 S. Roman St., New Haven, Conn. 06514). Center for Business Ethics, *A Collection of Business Ethics Syllabi,* 1982 (Center for Business Ethics, Bentley College, Waltham, Mass. 02254). Finally, Bond gives a fairly comprehensive list of sources that regularly publish articles in the area of business ethics and business moral values.

The literature being published in the area of business ethics is quite extensive and growing in leaps and bounds. Consequently, we would like to offer the brief and selected list of sources below as further suggested readings. We chose to include in this list many sources that tend to be more theoretical, philosophical, and in some cases, highly speculative, in the interest of complementing our more nuts-and-bolts, practical, or hands-on approach to problems in business ethics taken throughout the book.

ARTICLES

AAKER, DAVID A. and GEORGE S. DAY, "Corporate Response to Consumerism Pressures," *Harvard Business Review* (Nov-Dec 1972), pp. 112–114.

ARRINGTON, ROBERT L., "Advertising and Behavior Control," *Journal of Business Ethics,* Vol. 1, No. 1 (Feb. 1982), pp. 3–12.

BENN, STANLEY, "Freedom & Persuasion," in *Ethical Theory & Business,* (2nd ed.), eds. Tom L. Beauchamp and Norman E. Bowie. Englewood Cliffs, N.J.: Prentice-Hall, Inc., 1983.

BERGER, PETER L., "New Attack on the Legitimacy of Business," *Harvard Business Review* (Sept–Oct 1981), pp. 82–89.

BLACKSTONE, WILLIAM T., "The Search for an Environmental Ethic," in *Matters of Life & Death,* ed. Tom Regan. New York: Random House, Inc. 1980.

BLUMBERG, PHILLIP I., "Corporate Responsibility and the Employee's Duty of Loyalty and Obedience," in *Ethical Theory and Business,* pp. 304-316, eds. Tom L. Beauchamp and Norman E. Bowie. Englewood Cliffs, N.J.: Prentice-Hall, Inc., 1979.

CARSON, THOMAS L., R.C. WOKUTCH, K.F. MURRMAN, "Bluffing in Labor Negotiations: Legal and Ethical Issues," *Journal of Business Ethics,* Vol. 1, No. 1 (Feb. 1982), pp. 13–22.

CHAMPION, GEORGE, "Creative Competition," *Harvard Business Review* (May–June 1967), pp. 61–67.

COATS, JOSEPH F., "Computers and Business—A Case of Ethical Overload," *Journal of Business Ethics,* Vol. 1, No. 3 (1982), pp. 239–248.

DALTON, DAN R. and RICHARD A. COSIER, "The Four Faces of Social Responsibility," *Business Horizons,* Vol. 25, No. 3 (May–June 1982), pp. 19–27.

DRUCKER, PETER F., "Ethical Chic," *Forbes*, Sept. 14, 1981, pp. 160–173.

———, "Management's New Role," *Harvard Business Review* (Nov–Dec 1969), pp. 49–54.

ELLISTON, FREDERICK A., "Anonymity and Whistleblowing," *Journal of Business Ethics,* Vol. 1, No. 3 (1982), pp. 167–177.

———, "Civil Disobedience and Whistleblowing: A Comparative Appraisal of Two Forms of Dissent," *Journal of Business Ethics,* Vol. 1, No. 1 (Feb. 1982), pp. 23–28.

FINN, DAVID, "Struggle for Ethics in Public Relations," *Harvard Business Review* (Jan–Feb 1959), pp. 49–58.

FRENCH, PETER A., "The Corporation As A Moral Person," *American Philosophical Quarterly,* 16 (July 1979), pp. 207–215.

GILLESPIE, NORMAN C., "The Business of Ethics," *University of Michigan Business Review* (Nov 1975), pp. 1–4.

———, "Corporate Structures and Individual Freedom," in *Ethical Theory and Business,* pp. 348–352, eds. Tom L. Beauchamp, & Norman E. Bowie. Englewood Cliffs, N.J.: Prentice-Hall, Inc., 1979.

GOODPASTER, KENNETH E. & JOHN B. MATTHEWS, JR., "Can a Corporation Have a Conscience?" *Harvard Business Review* (Jan–Feb 1982), pp. 132–141.

GREEN, RONALD M., "Intergenerational Justice & Environmental Responsibility," pp. 334–342. *Right Conduct, Theories and Applications,* (1st ed.), eds. Michael D. Bayles & Kenneth Henley. New York: Random House, Inc. 1983.

GREYSER, STEPHEN A., "Advertising: Attacks and Counters," *Harvard Business Review,* Vol. 50, March 10, 1972, pp. 22–28.

GROSS, C.W. & HARRISH L. VERMA, "Marketing & Social Responsibility," *Business Horizons* (Oct. 1977).

HERMAN, NICKEL, "The Corporation Haters," *Fortune,* Vol. 101, No. 12, June 16, 1980, pp. 126–136.

HUGHES, J. DONALD, "Ecology in Ancient Greece," *Inquiry,* 18, pp. 115–125.

_______, "The Environmental Ethics of the Pythagoreans," *Environmental Ethics,* 2 (Fall 1980), pp. 195–214.

KONRAD, A. RICHARD, "Business Managers and Moral Sanctuaries," *Journal of Business Ethics,* Vol. 1, No. 3 (1982), pp. 195–200.

LEVITT, THEODORE, "The Morality (?) of Advertising," *Harvard Business Review* (July–Aug 1970), pp. 84–92.

LODGE, GEORGE CABOT, "Ethics and the New Ideology. Can Business Adjust?" *Management Review,* Vol. 66, No. 7 (July 1977), pp. 10–16.

_______, "The Connection Between Ethics and Ideology," *Journal of Business Ethics,* Vol. 1, No. 2 (May 1982), pp. 85–98.

MALKIEL, BURTON G., & RICHARD E. QUANDT, "Moral Issues in Investment Policy," *Ethical Theory and Business,* pp. 391–402, eds. Tom L. Beauchamp, & Norman E. Bowie. Englewood Cliffs, N.J.: Prentice-Hall, Inc., 1979.

NADER, RALPH, "Corporate Disclosure: The Public Right To Know," *Journal of Contemporary Business,* Vol. 7, No. 1 (Winter 1978), pp. 25–31.

NAGEL, THOMAS, "Equal Treatment and Compensatory Discrimination," *Philosophy and Public Affairs,* 2 (Summer 1973).

_______, "A Defense of Affirmative Action," *Ethical Theory and Business,* (2nd ed.), eds. Tom L. Beauchamp & Norman E. Bowie. Englewood Cliffs, N.J.: Prentice-Hall, Inc. 1983.

NAOR, J.F. & R.H. HUMANSON, "Wanted: A Code of Ethics For Internal Accountants," *Business,* Vol. 30, No. 6 (Nov–Dec 1980), pp. 12–17.

PARTRIDGE, ERNEST, "Are We Ready For An Ecological Morality?" *Environmental Ethics,* 4 (Summer 1982), pp. 175–190.

PASTIN, MARK & MICHAEL HOOKER, "Ethics and the Foreign Corrupt Practices Act," in *Ethical Theory and Business,* 2nd ed. eds. Tom L. Beauchamp and Norman E. Bowie. Englewood Cliffs, N.J.: Prentice-Hall, Inc. 1983.

POWERS, C.W. & D. VOGEL, *Ethics In The Education of Business Managers.* Hastings, N.Y.: Institute of Society, Ethics, and Life Sciences, 1980.

PURCELL, THEODORE V., S.J., "Do Courses in Business Ethics Pay Off?" *California Management Review,* XIX (Summer 1977), pp. 50–58.

_______, "Electing an 'Angel's Advocate' to the Board," *Management Review* (May 1976), pp. 4–11.

_______, "The Need for Corporate Ethical Specialists," *Review of Social Economy,* Vol. 36 No. 1 (April 1978), pp. 41–58.

RESCHER, NICHOLAS, "The Environmental Crisis," *Ethical Theory and Business,* pp. 558–562, eds. Tom L. Beauchamp & Norman E. Bowie. Englewood Cliffs, N.J.: Prentice-Hall, Inc., 1979.

SESSIONS, GEORGE, "Shallow & Deep Ecology: A Review of the Philosophical Literature," Robert C. Schultz and Donald Hughes, *Ecological Consciousness,* pp. 391–462. Washington, D.C.: University Press of America, 1981.

SINGER, PETER, "Rich and Poor," *Ethical Theory and Business,* 2nd ed., eds. Tom L. Beauchamp and Norman E. Bowie. Englewood Cliffs, N.J.: Prentice-Hall, Inc., 1983.

SOLOMON, KENNETH I. and HYMAN MULLER, "Illegal Payments: Where the Auditor Stands," *Journal of Accountancy* (Jan. 1977), pp. 51–57.

SPICER, BARRY H., "Accounting for Corporate Social Performance: Some Problems and Issues," *Journal of Contemporary Business,* Vol. 7, No. 1 (Winter 1978), pp. 151–170.

STERBA, JAMES P., "Welfare Rights of Future Generations," *Right Conduct, Theories and Applications,* 1st ed., eds. Michael D. Bayles and Kenneth Henley. New York: Random House, Inc. 1983.

WUTHROW, ROBERT, "The Moral Crisis in American Capitalism." *Harvard Business Review,* Vol. 60, No. 2 (March–April 1982), pp. 76–84.

BOOKS

ANSHEN, MELVIN, ed., *Managing the Socially Responsible Corporation,* New York: Macmillan Publishing Co., 1974.

BARRY, VINCENT, *Moral Issues In Business,* Belmont, CA.: Wadsworth Publishing Co., 1979.

BEAUCHAMP, TOM L., *Case Studies In Business, Society and Ethics,* Englewood Cliffs, N.J.: Prentice-Hall, 1983.

_______, & NORMAN E. BOWIE, eds., *Ethical Theory & Business,* 2nd ed., Englewood Cliffs, N.J.: Prentice-Hall, Inc., 1983.

BLACKSTONE, WILLIAM T., ed., *Philosophy and Environmental Crisis,* Athens: University of Georgia Press, 1974.

BOK, S., *Lying: Moral Choice In Public & Private Life,* New York: Pantheon Books, 1978.

BOWIE, NORMAN, *Business Ethics,* Englewood Cliffs, N.J.: Prentice-Hall, Inc., 1982.

BRAYBROOKE, DAVID, *Ethics In The World of Business,* Totowa, N.J.: Rowman & Allanheld, 1983.

DEGEORGE, RICHARD, *Business Ethics,* New York: Macmillan Publishing Co., Inc., 1982.

_______, and JOSEPH A. PICHLER, eds., *Ethics, Free Enterprise and Public Policy: Original Essays on Moral Issues in Business,* New York: Oxford University Press, Inc., 1978.

DONALDSON, THOMAS, *Case Studies in Business Ethics,* Englewood Cliffs, N.J.: Prentice-Hall, Inc., 1983.

_______, *Corporations and Morality,* Englewood Cliffs, N.J.: Prentice-Hall, Inc., 1982.

_______, & PATRICIA H. WARHANE, eds., *Ethical Issues In Business* (2nd ed.), Englewood Cliffs, N.J.: Prentice-Hall Inc., 1979.

EWING, DAVID, *Freedom Inside The Organization,* New York: McGraw-Hill, 1977.

GARRETT, THOMAS M., RAYMOND C. BAUMHART, THEODORE V. PURCELL, PERRY ROETS, *Cases In Business Ethics,* Englewood Cliffs, N.J.: Prentice-Hall, Inc., 1968.

GOODPASTER, K.E. & K.M. SAYER, eds., *Ethics and Problems of the 21st Century,* Notre Dame, Ind.: University of Notre Dame Press, 1979.

HERMAN, EDWARD S., *Corporate Control, Corporate Power,* New York: Cambridge University Press, 1982.

HOFFMAN, W. MICHAEL, ed., *Proceedings of the First National Conference on Business Ethics: Business Values and Social Justice: Compatibility on Contradiction,* Waltham, MA.: Bentley College, 1978.

_______, ed., *Proceedings of the Second National Conference on Business Ethics: Power and Responsibility in the American Business System,* Washington, D.C.: University Press of America, 1979.

_______, and THOMAS J. WILEY, eds., *Proceedings of the Third National Conference on Business Ethics: The Work Ethic in Business,* Cambridge, MA.: Oelgeschlager, Gunn and Hain, 1980.

_______, and JENNIFER MILLS MOORE, eds., *Proceedings of the Fourth National Conference on Business Ethics: Ethics and the Management of Computer Technology,* Cambridge, MA.: Oelgeschlager, Gunn and Hain, 1981.

_______, _______, *Business Ethics Readings and Cases in Corporate Morality,* New York: McGraw-Hill, 1984.

_______, _______, DAVID FEBO, eds., *Proceedings of the Fifth National Conference on Business Ethics: Corporate Governments and Institutionalizing Ethics,* Lexington, MA., Lexington Book, 1983.

MISSNER, MARSHALL, *Ethics of the Business System,* Sherman Oaks, CA.: Alfred Publishing Co., Inc., 1980.

NADER, RALPH & MARK J. GREEN, eds., *Corporate Power In America,* New York: Grossman Publishers, 1973.

PESKIN, HENRY M., PAUL R. PORTNEY, ALLEN V. KNEESE, eds., *Environmen-*

tal Regulation and the U.S. Economy, Baltimore: Johns Hopkins University Press, 1981.

PORTNEY, PAUL R., A. MYRICK FREEMAN III, ROBERT H. HAVEMAN, HENRY M. PESKIN, EUGENE M. SESKIN, V. KERRY SMITH, eds., *Current Issues In U.S. Environmental Policy* (3rd. ed.), Baltimore: Johns Hopkins University Press, 1980.

REGAN, TOM, *All That Dwell Therein: Essays on Animal Rights and Environmental Ethics,* Berkeley: University of California Press, 1982.

_______, ed., *Earthbound: New Introductory Essays in Environmental Ethics,* New York: Random House, 1983.

_______, ed., *Just Business: New Introductory Essays In Business Ethics,* New York: Random House, 1983.

_______, *The Case For Animal Rights,* Berkeley: University of California Press, 1983.

SIMON, JOHN, CHARLES POWERS, and JON GUNNERMANN, *The Ethical Investor: Universities and Corporate Responsibility,* New Haven, Conn.: Yale University Press, 1972.

SMITH, DAVID M., foreword by DAVID HARVEY, *Where The Grass Is Greener: Living In An Unequal World*, Baltimore: Johns Hopkins University Press, 1982.

SNOEYENBOS, MILTON, ROBERT ALMEDER, JAMES HUMBER, *Business Ethics,* Buffalo: Prometheus Books, 1983.

SOLOMON, ROBERT C. and KRISTINE R. HANSON, *Above the Bottom Line: An Introduction to Business Ethics,* New York: Harcourt, Brace Jovanovich, Inc., 1983.

VELASQUEZ, MANUEL G., *Business Ethics: Concepts & Cases,* Englewood Cliffs, N.J.: Prentice-Hall, Inc., 1982.

INDEX